# Alcan Trail Blazers

## Alaska Highway's Forgotten Heroes

D0810800

Home Sweet Home, Base Camp - Liard River, November 1942

Lt. Lancatser and his Recon crew at Ft. Nelson.

Scrubbing off some stink - Raspberry Creek 1942

D-8 Cat stuck... Again!

# Alcan Trail Blazers
## Alaska Highway's Forgotten Heros
Copyright 2005

Compiled by Earl L. Brown
Fort Nelson, BC

All rights reserved. Printed in Canada.
No part of the book may be used or reproduced in any manner whatsoever
without prior written permission except in the cases of brief quotations
embodied in critical articles or reviews.

Cover Design by Rod A. McLeod
Calgary, Alberta

Map inside front cover
Created by Cathy A Chapin - LakeHead University, Thunder Bay, Ont.

Editing Assistance
Leah Boltz, Don Edwards, Jennifer Ferguson, Stephanie Henry
Alex Kenyon, Wayne Mann, Carol Phillips, Kris Valencia

Technical Advisor and Page Design
Perry Everest Brown

Transcription of original letters and diaries
Helen L. Navratil, Mellissa Riley, Traci L. Rice

Typesetting
Traci L. Rice, Perry E. Brown

ISBN 0-9692380-4-5
April 2005

Printing - Quebecor World Jasper Printing
Suite 101, 11504 170 Street
Edmonton, Alberta Canada T5S 1J7
tel: 780-451-6750 fax: 780-451-4587 toll free: 800-661-3656

Published by

Box 904
Fort Nelson, BC V0C1R0
Tel: 250-774-3488 Fax: 250-774-6767
email: autumn@pris.ca
www.autumnimages.com

This book is dedicated to the men and families
of Company "A" 648th Topographical Battalion
United States Army 1942-1943

\* \* \*

To those who remain,
and to those who have gone before.

\* \* \*

Photographs, except where specially noted are
from the personal collections of members of the
648th Topographical Battalion
and their families.

# Alcan Trail Blazers
# Alaska Highway's Forgotten Heros
## *Including...*

*Harry Spiegel*
*...And his letters to home*

*Sid Navratil*
*...And his Alcan diaries*

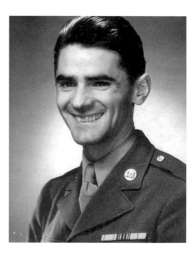

Chris Gras
... And his amusing anecdotes

My dear Mom & Dad,

How I wish that you could see
the beautiful scenery all about me,
as I sit here writing these few lines.
We are now in the heart of the
second range of the Rockies. The
higher mountains are bare rock
and well above timberline. On
cloudy days the higher peaks are
obscured in the swirling clouds,
and on clear, bright days they are
a most impressive sight, as
they stand as lonely sentinels
against a backdrop of deep blue
sky, reaching towards their
Creator. The river valley that we
are now working in is walled
in by a range of mountains on
either side. In many places there
are bad rock slides that come
right down to the rushing,
plunging river. Here the trail
hangs on the slides just above
the water's edge, and such places
prove pretty risky to bring a
pack outfit safely thru. A few
days ago, when an outfit was
passing along such a slide area
just below our present camp, 2
of the horses slid off a big,
slant rock and into the river.
They were toting packs and as
soon as they hit the water, the
current pulled them into the
river and they were carried
downstream. They began to swim,

# Contents

# INTRODUCTION AND ACKNOWLEDGEMENTS (BY EARL L. BROWN)

There's a lot of things that this book is not.

"Alcan Trail Blazers—Alaska Highway's Forgotten Heros" does not try to, or pretend to be a complete, authoritative and academic account of the building of the Alaska Highway. Good luck in trying to find such a book. Heath Twichell's "Northwest Epic, the building of the Alaska Highway" comes pretty close to filling that bill.

This book does not pretend to be a pictorial documentary of the highway's construction, brimming with myriad archival photographs. Stan Cohen of Pictorial Histories Publishing covers that area well with his many books, including "The Trail of '42, the Forgotten War series, and Alcan & Canol." Recently William Griggs, photographer with the 97th Engineers (one of the segregated regiments of black troops) produced "The World War II Black Regiment that helped build the Alaska Military Highway"—some exquisite photos.

This book has several photos, most of which were the personal snapshots taken by men of the 648th Topographical Battalion while preparing for, working on, or getting ready to leave the Alaska Highway campaign.

It's closer to the personalized accounts of guys who found themselves battling mud, muskeg and mosquitoes, like Chester L. Russell's "Tales of a Catskinner—A personal account of building the Alaska Highway, the Winter Trail and the Canol Pipeline Road in 1942-43." For a smorgasbord of stories from a variety of the cast of characters building the Alaska Highway, track down a copy of John T. Schmidt's "This Was No Friggin' Picnic—True Alaska highway construction tales," or perhaps David Remley's "The Crooked Road". There's a bunch more titles too, but enough about those books—this book flirts with aspects of all of the above.

Perhaps this book should be called "**Alcan Trail Blazers—Version II**".

Since the late 1970's, surviving veterans and family members of the 648th Topographical Battalion had been gathering annually at one place or another throughout the lower 48, depending on which member volunteered to host their reunion. Recognizing that 1992 marked the 50th anniversary of the construction of the Alaska Highway, and that in spite of the integral part that Company "A" played surveying a significant part of the road, since so darn little credit for their efforts was ever acknowledged, then perhaps the timing was right to create a book about the role they played, told by the men themselves in their own words. So that's exactly what they did.

Now, making a book happen is one heck of a lot of work. (Sometimes it's just as well people don't know how much work they're getting into ... could scare them off if they knew just how much was involved.) They persevered ... and eventually gave birth to the original, 64 page version of "Alcan Trail Blazers." It was hoped that profits from sale of this book could be used to create a monument somewhere along the Alaska Highway to recognize their arduous construction efforts. Unfortunately these profits, and subsequent monument, did not develop.

It is important to make readers aware of one individual who proved to be an amazing catalyst, and without her gentle urging and well timed prodding, this book would not have seen the light of day: Helen Navratil. Earlier Sid Navratil had made the effort to have his original diaries typed up for his children to appreciate the efforts of their father during WWII. He noted, "Without the persistent 'badgering' and encouragement of my wife, Helen, this diary of my war years would never have been published. To her this entire document is lovingly dedicated."

Later, a note of Sid's passing in 2002 was included in Chester Russell's book, "Tales of a Catskinner," and forwarded to Helen. Everything could have just ended there. But it didn't. A grateful Helen, as well as sending thanks for the book and for the mention, also sent a note to Harry Spiegel. Harry was one of the long legged, front of the pack surveyors, who had taken the time to write letters home to his folks during the campaign. Some excerpts from these letters were included in "Alcan Trail Blazers," but most remained unpublished. A collection of 56 typewritten pages of Alaska Highway history from "our backyard"—And could Harry ever write well! He had a gifted eye for detail and a wonderful way with words. Helen suggested that Harry send a copy of the summarized letters to one Earl Brown in Fort Nelson, Alaska Highway.

This collection of letters arrived in April 2003. Reading through them made the hair on the back of my neck stand up ... Amazing stuff! And then from Harry and his brother Carl in New York came more goodies and artifacts ... a hand drawn map from work on the Simpson Trail from Dec of '42, suggestions of other things that could be pursued before being lost for all time, and Harry's original WW1 vintage azimuth compass that he used while trailblazing for the highway. "You should try to contact Sgt. Chris Gras' daughter Karen in Colorado," they urged. "He had a home movie camera with him, and shot some film; it would sure be great if that could be saved..." From Karen Cecchinelli came a treasured assortment of maps, photos and wartime articles.

Fort Nelson Heritage Museum curator Marl Brown, holding Harry Spiegel's WWI vintage azimuth compass, used while building the Alaska Highway.

The Fort Nelson News was thrilled to "serialize" Harry Spiegel's "Letters to Home" and for five months running, readers could read the latest from Pvt. Harry Spiegel, 61 years after the fact. And what grand reading!

I showed Harry Spiegel's letters to Flo Whyard, author, former editor of "The Whitehorse Star," former Mayor of Whitehorse among other things. Flo doesn't mince words. "Those letters *have* to be published! They are an important part of the story of the Alaska Highway—and wonderfully written too."

Carol Urquart-Fisher of Dallas, Texas, sent along some three dozen photos from her father's collection. John Earl Fisher was the 648th's company clerk, and now, more never before published highway construction photos found their way back to near where they had been taken in the first place.

Importantly, some of the first nation guides, including Garnet Harrold and George Behn, who helped these trailblazers more than 60 years ago, are still around, and the opportunity to include their story in their own words adds a valuable insight into the overall construction experiences.

With the passage of time, some common phrases of the 1940's are no longer "politically correct." And that's how they remain in this book. Great care has been taken to ensure that original letters and correspondence are included exactly as written by the original authors. It is not the intention to offend any reader, nor is it the goal to provide a "revisionist history" sanitized version.

To all who read these following pages, whether your connection with the Alaska Highway spans back to the days of its original construction, or years before its "intrusion" into this land, or if like myself you've had opportunity in years gone by to travel every twisting dusty mile, or if you've only known the paved and groomed version of this historic road, I hope you have a better appreciation of its "birth" and the enormous contribution of those who made up the Alcan Trail Blazers, Alaska Highway's Forgotten Heros.

Earl L. Brown,
Fort Nelson, BC
April 2005

Just like the building of the Alaska Highway, the building of this book was not from the efforts of any one person, but rather a large and eclectic cast of characters, all of whom had their important part to play.

This includes, naturally, members and their families of Company "A" 648th Topographical Battalion. A huge debt of gratitude is due to Helen Navratil, the catalyst who helped bring many of the players together, the Spiegel "boys," Harry and Carl, and children of the Alcan soldiers, Karen Cecchinelli and Carol Urquart Fisher. Thanks is due also to Adolph Adrian, Ted Miduski and others of the original Alcan Trail Blazers who gave their blessing to go ahead with the revised book you now see, in spite of the fact that we have never yet met face to face. I hope that I have not let them down. They all seem like part of a terrific extended family.

On the home front, the huge contribution of my son Perry (what am I, your personal slave?) Brown is happily acknowledged, and support of my folks Marl & Mavis and my wife Sandy. Traci Rice contributed enormously to the project.

Thanks, too, to the Fort Nelson Historical Society who prepurchased some of the not yet printed books... and tolerated several revised completion dates. The wait was worth it, wasn't it.

From the original 1992 edition.
## A WORD FROM THE CONTRIBUTORS

We are indebted to the many people who made this book possible. Those who lived the great adventure of 50 years ago shared their photographs, diaries, letters home, and recollections, providing readers with first-hand accounts of a truly epic undertaking.

There were many others who also helped: Widows of men who are no longer with us, and those who gave both of time and effort in editing, illustrating, photo retouching, proofreading, printing and otherwise participating in the monumental task of putting this lasting record together.

| | | |
|---|---|---|
| Adolph Adrian | John A. Frank | Pete Pierce (Mildred) |
| Julius A. Anderson | James P. Gerardi | John Reagan |
| Norman E. Allen | Chris Gras | Joe Russac |
| John Blackmon | James Halfacre | John Shafer |
| Tom Brennan | Ira Kemp | Harry Spiegel |
| Stanley Caldwell | Ted Miduski | Paul Tiddens |
| Dan Dotta | Edward Montpetit | Floyd Weidman (Grace) |
| Alfred M. Eschbach | Sid Navratil | Joseph Wyhs |
| John Fisher | Charles Nesom | Mike Zintak |

Below are the names of the people who contributed, which identify their contributions. We apologize in advance for any that were inadvertently left out.

**EDITORIAL STAFF:** Sid Navratil, *Book Designer* / John Evans, *Photo Editor* Andrew Kovalik, *Cover Artist* / John Lloyd, Helen Navratil, Stan Caldwell, *Editors*.

**ADMINISTRATION:** Adolph Adrian, *Chairman, Board of Directors* Charles and Lahoma Smith, *Treasurers*.

# CHAPTER I

# MAJOR MIDUSKI'S SUMMARY

Following the Japanese attack on Pearl Harbor on December 7, 1941, it was feared that the western United States, Canada and Alaska were vulnerable to an invasion by the Japanese.

To meet this threat, President Franklin D. Roosevelt formed a special cabinet to consider the feasibility of building a road through Canada to Alaska as quickly as possible. Subsequently, the U.S. Army Corps of Engineers completed plans for the road in February 1942, and construction was authorized.

On March 2, 1942, "A" Company of the 648th Engineer Topographical Battalion left for duty on the Alaska Highway as part of Task Force 6968. Consisting of five officers and 156 enlisted men, it was one of two survey companies assigned the "task of locating, surveying and mapping the highway with all speed within the physical capacity of the troops."

Company "A" was assigned the section of the highway within the southern sector between Fort St. John, British Columbia, the northern terminus of existing roads, and Lower Post on the Liard River on the British Columbia–Yukon border, a distance of 600 miles. The mission was completed in November 1942.

During November and December of the same year, the company also located 256 miles of winter trail from Fort Nelson, British Columbia, to Fort Simpson, Northwest Territories, where the Liard River flows into the Mackenzie.

Its task completed, Company "A," with the exception of an officer and four enlisted men, left Canada in December and arrived at Camp McCoy, Wisconsin, on January 1, 1943.

The party of men left behind in Canada was ordered to locate an all-weather road from the Alaska Highway a few miles west of the settlement of Teslin, Yukon, extending northeast approximately 500 miles to Norman Wells, Northwest Territories, on the Mackenzie River. Between the middle of January and the end of February, 1943, these men braved temperatures as low as 60 degrees below zero and between five and seven feet of snow to locate 300-plus miles of the road, which was used in the construction of an oil pipeline from Norman Wells, Northwest Territories. At the end of February, Northwest Service Command released these men to their unit.

The construction of the Alaska Highway is one of the greatest wilderness undertakings in American history. It was an epic of engineering, not only because of the rugged terrain and weather conditions encountered but also because the 1,600 mile highway was completed in less than nine months.

This book is dedicated to the men of "A" Company, 648th Engineer Topographic Battalion, whose courage, fortitude and ingenuity helped make it possible. We take pride in our motto, "The Elite." And this, in our words and pictures, is our story.

Theodore A. Miduski
Major (Retired)
U.S. Army

...never ending mud!

Shafer and Horner on the plane-table.

# CHAPTER II

# CAMP CLAIBOURNE, LOUISIANA

In early February 1942, I received a telegram from the office of Brig. Gen. Clarence Sturdevant, Assistant Chief of Engineers, U.S. Army, which read:

**YOU WILL TAKE ONE COMPANY OF MEN AND PROCEED TO DAWSON CREEK, BRITISH COLUMBIA, AND THENCE IN A NORTHWESTERLY DIRECTION TO FAIRBANKS, ALASKA, LOCATING A ROUTE FOR A MILITARY ROAD.**

When the assignment to the Alaska Highway came through, I was a 27 year-old captain commanding Company "A" 648th Topographic Battalion of the U.S. Army Corps of Engineers, Louisiana. We had a month to prepare for departure.

Alfred M. Eschbach

**Extracts from Sid Navratil's Diary**

*February 17, 1942        Tuesday*

*My luck is changing (after yesterday). Today I received my specialist rating; Sp. Fourth Class. That means I will be drawing $45 a month, but not until I've finished my first four months in the army. Till then I'll continue to draw $21. Boy, can I use that money, too! My Tech bills are coming home every month, and I'm going to try to take care of them. One can live very cheaply here. Last week I spent a little over a dollar now that I "roll my own." However, this advancement means more to me than just the money; it proves to me that with little effort one can get ahead pretty fast; and with this incentive, I'm going to try some more.*
*I yearn for letters from home, and from friends—from Helen.*
*Lights out.*

*February 23, 1942     Monday*

*This was a typical Louisiana day; the sky was overcast as we "fell out" at 6:30, and then at 8 it began to pour, filling the streets with running water. With the lunch hour the storm passed away, so that in the afternoon we could enjoy one of the best bits of weather of the season.*

*President Roosevelt is to speak tonight; it will be his second "fireside chat" since Pearl Harbor. No doubt he will stress again the urgency to "get down to business," as well as explaining the reason why the Army took over the business of getting rid of the enemy aliens.*

*February 25, 1942     Wednesday*

*It's shortly after noon now, and the camp is buzzing with rumors. Latrine rumor No.1952 has it that we are "moving out," it will probably be an alert again. Everything is packed, and we're waiting for the whistle. Today I started drawing my $1.50 a day, which is the only thing that sounds good to me now.*

*February 26, 1942     Thursday*

*The battalion exodus began today. At the rate we were going today, we all would soon be muscle-bound. At four o'clock we had another orientation lecture, this time delivered by a columnist-ambulance driver who had seen action in France when the Germans took the well-known bridge at Sudan. It was a vivid description: told by a man whose appearance gave authenticity to his statements, the story gave me an inside glimpse into the tortured, frightened France. He disputed all claims that France was corrupt and cowardly. It was simply a matter of unheard of ingenuity and cunning of the Germans, who had been preparing and planning this attack for over twelve years.*

*March 1, 1942     Sunday*

*Twenty-four hour guard duty yesterday and today. Up to today, this was undoubtedly my worst Sunday. In a driving rain that penetrated our raincoats and filled our shoes, we stood guard in four two-hour shifts.*

*We are on the move again (that is certain) . Only this time it is to be far, far away, probably somewhere in the Arctic regions—if the fur lined clothing to be issued means anything. What hurts is that we are to carry the least amount of personals, which means my radio, my watercolors, tablets, and perhaps the camera also. I'm going to do my darnest best to smuggle the latter with me.*

*March 2, 1942     Monday*

*Our Arctic clothing has been issued to us today. Uncle Sam spent $450 on each of us to keep us warm "over there." I'm wishing we would start out soon as I* *want to know where we're going.*

*It's 8 p.m. now and we're waiting for another formation; probably more clothing. The captain told us one pair of boots we were issued costs around $45!*

*I wrote home to Helen, and there was a lump in my throat, as I'm afraid I won't see them all for a long, long time to come.*

*March 4, 1942　　　　Wednesday*

*We worked in the rain all day, crating, painting and otherwise getting ready for the departure. Two fellows were sent to the guardhouse for being late at last night's 7 o'clock formation. Right now the trucks are all loaded, ready for instant departure. Some say it's to be the Canadian Rockies, and at this time of year it must be around -50 degrees there!*

Special equipment was rushed in by express train to Claibourne and it was impressed upon the men by Captain Eschbach as to the precious value of time in our operations. The full complement of officers was also completed and they were headed by Captain A. E. Eschbach, aided by Lieutenants C. Nesom, M. R. Stewart, F. J. Hoppe and L. S. Lancaster, Jr. They immediately obtained the confidence and were quite popular with all the men. However, with all due respect, it may be added that there was never a dull moment with Captain Eschbach about.

Unattributed, *"Of Maps and Men"*

While getting ready to leave Camp Claibourne for Canada, there were promotions and transfers so that some of the G.I.'s could form other companies. They eventually went to Australia, while Co. "A" got ready to leave for Canada.

One of the Captains had me go to one of our warehouses and check for explosives that were to go with us. I went to the warehouse and found a large pile of boxes wrapped in red flagging. After untying the large bundle, I found four cases of TNT, a roll of regular fuse, and a roll of instantaneous fuse topped with a box of dynamite caps. It scared me to death even after I removed the caps.

I then checked with Sgt. Jennerjahn to see if he was nuts. He was upset until we took the caps to the main office, where the officers were afraid to put them in the Company safe. Finally, Adolph Adrian said that "Jennerjahn and I should know what they are doing," and put them in the safe. The rest of the explosives were loaded on the train in their regular boxes, properly labelled.

Chris Gras

*March 6, 1942　　　　Camp Claiborne, LA*

*Today all of the fellows in our outfit, having hand luggage, boxes, and parcels to be sent home, turned them all in to a storeroom.*

*We are warned to keep the knowledge of our pending trip and mission a secret. Oddly enough, much date and information about it was heard a number of times in news flashes over the radio cast last night to the general public. It struck me as being rather humorous. We were told by our captain we are going into the wilderness far from towns and civilization, and there would be very little opportunity to spend money. It still is just a matter of a handful of hours before "Toot, Toot."*

*Harry Spiegel*

Getting ready for our "Northern adventure."

NCO's Warlikowski, Weidman
and Graves take five.

# CHAPTER III

# ON THE TRAIN TO DAWSON CREEK

### From Harry Spiegel's Letters Home

*March 8, 1942*                       *Aboard a train*

*Well, we are finally on our way. We left camp yesterday afternoon. I try to console myself, because many of these fellows who haven't been home or seen their folks in many months, were cheated of their promised furloughs, some only a few days before they were due to get leaves.*

*Shortly after boarding, we were told henceforth all letters will be censored. We are forbidden to disclose our destination, facts concerning the mission or organization, names of the towns and cities passed thru and any details of our trip.*

*Quite appropriately, we left camp yesterday in a drizzle and it has been raining and gloomy since. As I gaze from my Pullman window, the landscape is water-bogged and puddled wherever I look. What dismal weather.*

*Under the difficulties of cooking over portable gasoline ranges in a baggage car, the meals are O.K.*

*March 10, 1942*                      *Aboard a train*

*As the wonders and the vastness of our great country unfold as we roll along, again I realize this region is truly the "breadbasket of our nation."*

*March 12, 1942*                      *Aboard a train*

*This afternoon completes the fifth consecutive day and night of traveling, and we are still not at our destination, however, I expect our journey to be over soon. Last night we left the Canadian plains behind, and now are rolling thru brush and timber country. This section is sparsely inhabited and most of these people live in mud chinked log cabins. Many of the inhabitants here are Indians who live very primitively and simply. It doesn't appear these natives know practically the whole world is aflame with war.*

*Vast lakes dot the map of this area. Lumbering, mink raising and fishing seem to be the chief occupations. These people live a hearty existence in a rugged territory. There are no signs of spring here yet. It is now gently snowing, but it is not too cold. All the rivers and lakes are still icebound. The folks in the little towns seem to be expecting us, because they all turn out and wave as we pass. Our train has stopped and I am going to step off and get a few lungs full of this crisp, pine, northern air.*

## Extracts from Sid Navratil's Diaries

*March 8, 1942          Sunday*

*We had quite a hectic day of it yesterday, but did get started eventually at 3:45 p.m. Our troop train is not too comfortable; our overcoats, belts and rucksacks hanging everywhere; air-conditioning is almost nil, so the air isn't the best, either. We live on strict rations that must last 20 days or more, so it's always plenty of grumbling when-ever the "mess" comes around.*

*I finished my KP duty on the train, peeling spuds most of the time, while the train hiccuped and jerked spasmodically. The kitchen car is a baggage car, not too clean, with floors that have never been scrubbed. We scoured it four or five times but it still looks dirty...*

*Outside the scenery is dull level country with pasteboard shacks and barns. And this dullness is heightened by a continuous drizzle that started when we left yesterday.*

*We have been standing here for half an hour or so; there was a train wreck up ahead and we've been waiting for the tracks to clear. Just now we've begun to move again and it stopped again! It's 10 a.m. and the road sign outside tells me this is Arkansas.*

*Tomorrow it will be two months since my departure from Belvoir to Claibourne.*

*We passed the wreck—it had been a head-on collision of freight trains— and it was quite a mess. Perhaps it was intended for another train... The rain has turned to sleet, and tomorrow at this time we should have entered the snow country.*

*8 p.m—We passed through fertile Illinois valleys and marshes—and are now entering St. Louis. The cars are hot and stuffy; it's difficult to breathe even. We may go to Chicago before Seattle; but then, no one knows.*

*March 9, 1942          Monday*

*This morning we entered Burlington, Iowa, invading the depot restaurant and "cleaning out" all the eatables. The landscape consists of fertile rolling farm land. Cottony cumulus clouds move slowly in the sky. Whenever we pass through a town, the people come out and wave to us; some give us the "V" sign or the "thumbs up" gesture—they all seem glad to see us.*

*3:45 p.m. We have traveled for 48 hours now. There are patches of snow, and some marshy places are frozen over. Iowa is the home state of many of our men and they're all quite enraptured by the sight of it—and proud, too, and rightly so. By the sun the watch shows that we're traveling north-west, taking me further from home than I've ever been before.*

*March 10, 1942          Tuesday*

*10 a.m. Somewhere in Minnesota.*

*For hours now we haven't seen anything that even resembles a hill. There is snow on the ground, and the streams are covered with ice. As for the soil, this is one of the richest states in the Union. Soon now we will be leaving the good old USA.*

*2 p.m.—We're in Canada now, having crossed the border at 1:15 p.m. Some women were there with a basket full of cigarettes—enough for everyone. Outside, white expanse of snow. It's snowing now and the sky and land blend into one...*

*Moving North*

*March 11, 1942          Wednesday*

*1:30 p.m. Saskatoon, Canada*

*Another rush to the depot, candy bars, coffee and donuts, magazines. People asking if we're American soldiers. Back on the train again. Outside, the snow is melting in the warm sunshine. Flat, unbroken country.*

*7 p.m. Alberta, Canada*

*Thousands of acres of flat grass-lands. In the distance the snow glistens in the golden light. Towns are few and far between. A herd of horses, half-wild, stands still, the manes blowing in the wind.*

Passing through Edmonton, Alberta.

*March 12, 1942          Thursday*

*What a change! This morning we were greeted by the wild north-west. Frozen lakes, their white enhanced by the evergreens. It is snowing now, and from the looks of the sky, will continue to do so for a long time to come. In about an hour's time we counted fifty jack-rabbits—all of them white to make them hardly discernible from the snow. There are rumors of "ba'ars" in this country.*

*In Edmonton the newspapers carried a headline about our mission—the Alaska Road—which was supposed to be a secret military mission. There were maps, too.*

*It's 7 p.m. now, and the sun is on the horizon. The sky is cloudless over-head, but on the ridge it rolls in billowy bundles. The train is led by two engines now, as we are in the foothills of the Canadian Rockies; from now on the going will be slow, and sometime tonight (or morn) we will reach the end of the RR line—Dawson Creek. From then on we shall travel in trucks until we reach the end of the trail—from then on, it will be up to us to continue from where man left off...*

*5:30 a.m.—We seem to be on the top—or the roof—of the world. Its -5 degrees and cold as hell! And today we unload!*

Heading for Dawson Creek and cold as hell!

# CHAPTER IV

# DAWSON CREEK TO SET UP AT CAMP ALCAN

### From Harry Spiegel's Letters Home

*March 16, 1942*                    *Fort St. John, British Columbia, Canada*

*Company A of the 648th Engineer Topographic Battalion arrived at the railhead, Dawson Creek, British Columbia, in the morning of March 13.*

*We are now located on the last fringe of civilization; 60 miles from the   nearest railroad and there are no roads save for one bush trail blazed about 300 miles north to Fort Nelson from here. In plain sight of the towering, challenging snow-capped peaks of the rugged Canadian Rockies our work begins. What a magnificent, soul-stirring sight these mountains are! Only in my wildest fancies did I ever dream I would be able to behold the beauties of this nature-laden country.*

*For two days and nights, four other fellows and I were stationed back at Dawson Creek guarding some of our equipment at a railhead. While off duty Saturday night, four of us went into town for a few hours. First, we headed for a restaurant. I had a porterhouse steak that hung two inches over the edges of my platter and it melted in my mouth. The meal included all the trimmings, including dessert. What a feed for 70 cents. Our dollar is worth $1.10 up here. This is quite a novelty for the boys. What a frontier town Dawson Creek is! Square-fronted western type stores and buildings line the one, muddy, rutted Main Street of the town. There are very few automobiles and horses are a very popular mode of transportation. There is a hitching post in front of every business establishment. These towns would make an ideal movie set for a western thriller. What characters these folks are! They are rough and tough, but very friendly, and anxious to chat with us. We ambled about town Saturday night and joked with the gals and waitresses in the cafes.*

*Yesterday, we fellows and the equipment were picked up and came north to a camp here just outside of the settlement of Fort St. John. It was a most interesting trip and a thrilling experience to cross the Peace River on the ice, reported to be about 5 feet thick. What a beautiful gorge the river flows in, with large mountainside plunging down to the floor of the Peace River valley! The terrific pressure of the river under the ice has caused a jumble of piles of up heaved packed-ice. What an exciting ride between the packs across the river on the ice. As we climbed the mountain on the north side of the Peace, another large army outfit in convoy, almost fly-like in size in the distance, made an unusual spectacle as it slowly moved across the river thru the pack ice.*

*We all have our complete Arctic outfits out, and when I get it all on, I can hardly move, but am as warm as toast.*

*March 18, 1942          Fort St. John, British Columbia, Canada*

*My five tent mates and I are sitting around our little stove in the candlelight as I write. Each of the six fellows hail from a different State and from a different section of our country. They are mighty fine companions. One chap is an Iowa farmer, another a very religious fellow from Detroit, a lobster fisherman from Boston, a Californian, a petroleum engineer from Texas(our Corporal) and the last, me, an Ebenezer onion! In this Company there are undoubtedly some of the finest fellows I have met in the Army.*

*Base camp here is pretty well organized, and except for hauling a few cords of wood, we had the afternoon to ourselves, so all six of us took to washing our dirty clothes in a very limited supply of water in dish pans on the straw floor of the tent. You should see our tent tonight! With all the zig-zagged lines overhead, it looks like "Hogan's Alley."*

*This morning we had a most beautiful sunrise! For some time the whole eastern sky was a brilliant cherry red, heralding the birth of a new day unspoiled and unmarked by man and war. And then, turning to the west, what a magnificent sight I beheld! The atmosphere was unusually clear and in the bright rays of the sun the majestic Canadian Rockies, reaching towards God crystal white in appearance, made a most imposing, thrilling sight!*

*March 19, 1942          Fort St. John, British Columbia, Canada*

*Many convoys of heavy engineering and pontoon boat equipment are arriving every day. This section has never seen so much excitement and activity in all its history. Even though I am in the midst of army activity all around me, all this impresses me as if I were working on a huge, peacetime construction job, or a member of a wilderness expedition. Very few war time precautions are observed. Open fires burn at night, no camouflage is used and the trucks do not use their blackout lights. I saw some more detailed accounts about this job in a newspaper in the beanery last night.*

*The ground is still frozen so hard the trench for the latrine had to be dynamited with a number of charges. It is impossible to use a pick ax.*

*Southwesterly winds from the slopes of the distant mountains are prevalent. Our Captain stated the most distant peaks are about 140 miles from here!*

*Corporal Haliburton, the tall, redheaded Texan, saw a tentative schedule, which indicated he and I were two members of a four-man recon-naissance squad. That promises to be an interesting detail, because we will act as an advance group. Our Company is going to work on the southern sector of this tremendous job, working north. It is rumored pack horses are going to be pressed into service on this job too. In order to avoid the boggy muskeg lying ahead, the proposed road is going to be staked along the sides and over the mountains. What beauty lies ahead! The natives claim in the summer the mosquitoes up in the muskeg are as big as an ordinary fingernail!*

## Extracts from Sid Navratil's Diary

*March 14, 1942          Saturday                    Ft. St. John, B. C. Canada*

*We went through one of our most trying days—and nights—yesterday. At 9:30 a.m. we started unloading, a job that lasted till 3:30 p.m. And then the trip to camp began a trip that all of us will long remember. There were about twenty-four of us in the large GI truck. Except for the overcoats, our clothing at this time was of the summer variety, and many an unkind word was said as we sat there, frigid from the cold. The ride lasted for about six hours, and most of it was in total darkness as we pulled down the tarpaulin. It's almost impossible to describe the variety of feel-ings of a group of men who, without seeing each other, feel the others' presence and, as the truck careens on an icy road, feel the others' fears... And when a steep climb would begin, we all would be silent breaking into a relieved, hard-to-conceal nonchalant speech. And upon arriving, we found a few hastily pitched tents, to which we brought our army cots—and of course, our sleeping bags. The sky was magnificent with the northern lights—aurora borealis—that moved and quivered across the heavens. The night was cold to the utmost, and we felt it most in the morning. But after changing into our new clothing, all shivering soon disappeared, and we were perspiring from the work. And there was plenty of that.*

*With the sunshine we were able to see our surroundings. Up to the north-west we can see, some 100 miles away (its clear here!) the majestic white Rockies. They're like giant cones and cubes of ice, beautiful from the distance. Before we come to them however, we will have to cross over two hundred miles of muskeg.*

*I heard the word "muskeg" for the first time yesterday, and I think I shall say much about it from now on. In Russia, it is known as "tundra;" in Europe and America they say "quicksand," but none seem to compare to this. In winter it is frozen over, and we shall be able to travel on it in our trucks, but when the spring comes, we will be stranded on the opposite side, with the Rockies and the muskeg separating us from the world. We are taking 150 days provisions with us, so it will not be easy. Even so, not one of us would trade this with the easy life in Claibourne. In a speech today, the captain emphasized the fact that a number of us will not come out at all—but then, this is a war, and we're taking the usual risks of "expendables."*

*March 15, 1942          Sunday*

*We worked all day today, setting up our new camp. Evidently we will stay here for a few days before we start out for Fort Nelson. It's a little too cold for writing tonight.*

*March 17, 1942          Tuesday*

*I found my pen again. It's hard writing in pencil.*

*A strong gale, accompanied by snow, shook our tents during the night. And in the morning all that slop and mud that covered the area was frozen hard, and was covered with a fine blanket of snow. Yesterday, the 74th (Light Pontoon) Eng. Battalion moved in, and there I saw again one of our "gang" from Belvoir, Housend. His only past-time, he says, is writing, and it helps him a great deal.*

*Lower down the road, the 35th makes their camp. As I went to the woods to chop some trees, I spoke to a "traffic guard" who was directing the traffic at the crossroads. Their parkas are not as warm as ours, and he was shivering in the biting sunshine.*

*It's lunchtime almost, and this morning there was little to do. A garbage hole and a new latrine dug in the hard-as-rock earth takes all day for a crew of men. With dynamite charges the job is somewhat lessened, but the explosive, too, is rationed out.*

*March 18, 1942          Wednesday*

*The pen is misbehaving—it must be the frost. When we get to colder climate, I must remember to empty it every night.*

*A day's KP for me again today. All morning the water would freeze on the pots as I washed them outside. The hands are sore from the continuous change from hot to cold... We had a brief snow storm today; for at least half an hour we could see it move across the "white peaks," descending down into the valley, and then continuing blowing in the south-easterly direction. It almost missed us; when the snow fell, the sun was shining brightly. Of course, there was no rainbow, but I couldn't help looking for it.*

*A convoy of trucks left for Fort Nelson, carrying provisions. They will be gone for at least four days, so we have at least that many days left to stay here at our present camp.*

*The boys are running like wild to the town (some 3 miles away) taking their last "fling" at life; eating steak dinners, running after women of all races and colors, and otherwise "shining" while they have the chance. We found out today that mail and our pay will be dropped to us from planes—we shall not be able to write, however.*

*March 21, 1942          Saturday*

*First day of Spring!*

*It's still snowing pretty hard, and the temperature is down to zero. We have been getting ready to move out today. One group goes to Ft. Nelson, while the other is staying. I am going, and it is a 25 hr. drive. It's going to be a hard trip, and at the end of it we'll find nothing but hard labor. But here goes...*

No one will ever forget that ride to Fort St. John, as at dusk the thermometer was rapidly dropping, making the steel-bottomed trucks anything but comfortable. It seemed that we would never reach there and what with the trucks sliding and slipping, whining and chattering, the whole scene took on a nightmarish aspect. The colder it got, the more the men stamped, moaned and cursed.

However, the trucks all crossed in safety and arrived at Fort St. John and the rosy picture we conjured up of a small outpost where hot coffee and food were awaiting us, rapidly dissipated. It took exactly five seconds and we were through town before we realized the trucks were not stopping. Some hardy soul raised the ice-covered canvas flap, looked out and saw the rapidly disappearing Fort was nothing but a few frame buildings. If we were rather disillusioned at this point it was tame to what we experienced later. For, after bumping and bouncing on an old wagon trail, we pulled into a snow-covered field and stopped.

It was now approximately 11 o'clock, and we clambered out of the trucks half frozen.

There were tents set up, including an improvised kitchen. Price, O'Brien, Kemp, Police, and the rest of the cooks had worked hours in setting up the field stoves, laboring long and hard all night that we might have a half-hot half-cold cup of coffee and a bite to eat. They deserve much credit in the work they accomplished through those long hours under the most trying conditions. The temperature dropped to -38 degrees below zero during the night.

The next morning as we put on the cold clothing we died a thousand deaths. Bare feet stamped about the snow, and the air was blue with cursing. "Will we ever feel warm again?" someone asked, over and over again.

Unattributed, *"Of Maps and Men"*

## "THIS IS WHERE YOU SLEEP"

We set up our permanent camp in Fort St. John, which had a population of roughly 500. It was about 30 degrees below zero, and there was light snow falling, whipped by a brisk wind. The ground was frozen as hard as flint. At this site I lined up the company and said "OK, men, this is where you sleep." It was impossible to drive in wooden tent stakes, so we made holes for the stakes by driving a steel spike, putting in the tent stakes and pouring water over them. The water froze so hard that there was no possibility of the stakes coming out. The first night we got eight tents, and we all crowded into those tents to await the dawn.

Alfred M. Eschbach

Camp Alcan - Fort St. John, B.C.

## DIARY JOTTINGS

Arrived at Dawson Creek Friday, March 13th. Loaded trucks for the trip to Fort St. John. Arrived nearly frozen. Convoy crossed Peace River on ice. Camp set up 3-1/2 miles NW of Fort St. John. Got up this morning with ice all over my sleeping bag. Two trucks dropped through the ice: 4 men drowned.

Mud three inches deep everywhere. So tired, it's as though I were drunk. Started building frame for hospital. Post hard to put down in mud. Haven't been out in the field yet. Helped set out foundation of 2 headquarters, 2 hospitals, and a warehouse. Brown and Pierce saw a bear. Brown had shells, but no gun. Pierce had a .45 and two shells, but didn't take the chance of only wounding the bear.

Edward Montpetit

# CHAPTER V

# WINTER RUSH TO FORT NELSON

**From Harry Spiegel's Letters Home**

*March 24, 1942*          *Fort Nelson, British Columbia, Canada*

*Our advance party, only 43 in number, is now set up in a snug little camp on a bluff overlooking the ice-bound Muskwa River. I am quite comfortable sitting here on my cot in the warmth of the Sibley stove in our tent in the glow of a freshly lit candle.*

*We left Fort St. John last Saturday night about 10 o'clock in a blustery snow-storm. There were five of us in the back of the truck to start with. What an experience our trip proved to be! The trip took us almost 30 hours. On the map just a bush trail is indicated for the 280 miles between Fort St. John and Fort Nelson, and it really isn't much more. After a few trips like that it's a miracle these army trucks aren't all ready for the junk pile. They sure are built to take it! Some of the grades were so steep the trucks had to be pulled up the hills with teams or caterpillar tractors, even though our trucks were in 4-wheel drive and had lugging chains on all four wheels. Often we slid off the trail and had to pull the trucks onto the road again with a winch, standard equipment on all these trucks. The way we hit some of the chuckholes, it's a wonder the truck I was riding in had a nut and bolt left in it when completing our journey. With winding, rough trail, steep hills, frosty windshields, and lack of sleep, the drivers shore had a tough assign-ment. After we were on our way a few hours, it stopped snowing and, as the stars twinkled in the cold sky and the Northern lights flashed and shim-mered, the thermometer took a toboggan ride. Except for a few GI wafers, we had no grub en route. That was someone's oversight, however.*

*Fortunately we had our heavy all-wool comforters to cover ourselves with on the trip. It was so cold our whiskers and the comforters around our necks were white with frost from our breath. Many of the fellows suffered from cold feet during the trip. It was 20 below zero when we pulled in here about one o'clock Monday morning. Even though the fur around my hooded parka was frosty from my breath, and my nostrils kind of stuck together when taking a deep breath, I didn't realize it was that cold. Thank goodness, they have a dry, still cold up here. Many of the boys had their socks and innersoles frozen to the bottom of their shoe pacs when we finally arrived. One poor chap froze all his toes on one foot during the trip. When he removed his shoe, all his toes and part of his foot was a blackish blue. He was flown back to the field hospital at Fort St. John yesterday. It is rumored gangrene had already set in and amputation will be necessary.*

*A dog team pulled in here yesterday. Seven huskies pulled a very light, streamlined mushing sled driven by a Canadian policeman clad in a very showy Arctic outfit. Their outfits sure were a novelty for us. Those dogs are well trained, but don't seem very pleased with their job. As soon as they would get the order to stop, all would flop down in the snow with a bored expression on their faces. They liked to be petted and fussed with by the soldiers. Their harnesses had bells on them and as they trotted along, they jingled so prettily. An average well-trained dog is supposed to be worth about $250. There is an outfit of construction engineers here, too. You should see the rations. They are stacked up in piles like cord wood, a pleasant sight in this wilderness of dense stands of Norwegian spruce and tall, gray quaking aspen. Our chow is very good and a fellow can always get "seconds."*

*There was a Fox Movietone cameraman up here today taking pictures of the activities going on. We are now situated about 5 miles outside of the settlement of Fort Nelson, which has a total of nine buildings—mostly trading posts.*

The first of the US troops arrived at Fort Nelson, March 1942.
On hand is 16 year old George Behn with his dog team.
(Photo courtesy of George Behn)

*March 26, 1942*                              *Camp near Fort Nelson,*
                                             *British Columbia, Canada*


*Eleven of us, including an officer and a cook, are now preparing and will start very shortly on a month's reconnaissance trip in a northwesterly direction. Our group will be the first party to head into the wilderness from here. Although dangerous, I am happy to be one of the party going out on this advanced mission. The lieutenant in charge is a fine friendly character and the boys are all swell chaps.*

*I never dreamed that I would have the opportunity to explore this rugged country as a member of a surveying expedition of this kind. Fate has dealt friendly with me so far in the army during this terrible war. I haven't seen a newspaper headline, heard a news broadcast or even any conversation about current events in the outside world in so long that can't realize that a world wide war is raging on scores of battle fronts at this very moment. Up here we never think about being attacked, bombed or gassed. I haven't handled my pistol in a dog's age. Instead of an enemy, only the silent, unspoiled beauties of nature abound up here in any direction one gazes. Words miserably fail to describe the scenery and the experiences that I've had in this "God's Country" so far.*

*Although at night the temperature is about zero, during the day the bright sunshine is ideal. Even though the snow and ice doesn't melt any, I am able to go about without a coat, hat or mittens and feel very comfortable. It is truly an ideal, healthful climate. During the cold snap (which I wrote about on the 24th) two truck drivers froze to death and were found rigidly slumped over the steering wheels of their vehicles. It was reported to be 30 below that night. We haven't heard how in our organization that froze the toes and part of his foot during our frigid journey up here is making out. We got our finger crossed for him.*


*April 2, 1942*                              *Camp near Fort Nelson,*
                                             *British Columbia, Canada*


*Our present camp overlooks the Muskwa River, still solidly ice-bound, and winding beautifully through the heavy timber. We are still waiting for the announcement of definite plans to start out on reconnaissance, survey missions and to start work on the road. Although the weather has been ideal during the last week, tonight it has taken a turn for the worse, and it is snowing intermittently again.*


*April 5th, 1942*                            *Camp near Fort Nelson*


*On Good Friday it began to snow, and continued on and off through Saturday until a fresh white four-inch mantel covered all the landscape. By closely examining the flakes as they fell on one's coat sleeve, almost every-*

one resembled perfect six pointed stars or delicate lace-like patterns. I never noticed such beauty in snowflakes before. How marvelous and perfect nature is! The tall, spired spruces are particularly beautiful with their fresh snow-laden boughs. The woods are so quiet and far away from civilization when one walks off into them, a hush seems to fall over them, causing one to tread in reverence.

Good Friday morning, a survey party started out in three Carry-alls (GI station wagons)over a rough trail through big timber down on to the ice crossing the Muskwa River. We had to take river soundings up and down stream from the cross-over itself. After necessary reference and tie-in, survey lines were established on each shore in lines parallel to the main channel of the river, we proceeded to chop holes through the ice at 10-foot intervals all the way across the stream on a line both above and below the crossing. The average ice on the Muskwa is about 18" thick, but it is starting to get a little spongy in places. The sounding in the middle of the river measures the channel at about eight and a half deep, and mighty fast water, too.

We have been issued a new type of pot-bellied stove for our tents. They throw a nice steady heat. We also have a newer, safer type of spark arrestor on our stovepipes. If the old type wasn't clogging and causing our tents to become filled with smoke, it was emitting sparks and burning holes in many of the tents.

Yesterday afternoon a buddy from Georgia and I were detailed to go over to the Quartermaster Field Bakery as fire stokers for the outdoor ovens and to work in the mixing tent. According to the duty roster it was our turn. We reported at 5 p.m. and were there until the last batch was baked off about 5 o'clock this morning. We chopped enough wood for the night by dusk, and from then on it was easy. I did the firing. The two outdoor ovens look crude, but are very effective. I had to hold them at a baking temperature of 550 degrees F. The four baker lads on duty were all bakers in civilian life, and sure are cracker jacks. You should see them work out the vats dough. They can shape up fancy pastry like machines. First they made a pan of delicious fruit cobbler for ourselves. We tackled it as soon as it left the oven and cooled a little. I never tasted such a delicacy in my life. During the earlier hours of the night a number of officers stopped in the bakery and sampled the tempting tid-bits. The bakers "run off" a number of different kinds of sweet rolls and 144 loaves of bread during the night. A welcome pot of coffee is always handy on the stove. Those baker boys, although pale, are husky from wrestling dough around. A GI loaf of bread is round like pumpernickel and is about a foot in diameter. A four and half pound chunk of dough comprises a kneaded loaf as it hits the bake pan ready for the oven. Each oven contains 36 loaves to a bake. What a delicious aroma is emitted from the oven during the process! Powdered milk is used in all of the baking.

*April 10, 1942*                    *Camp near Fort Nelson*

*Every day this week, directly after breakfast, a few reconnaissance and plane-table parties have loaded equipment, jumped in carry-all trucks, and headed northwesterly into the wilderness as far as we are able to go. The four of us in our party have been heading through the wilderness on a compass bearing towards a spot designated on an aerial photograph as Evelyn Lake. I doubt if man has ever set foot or even gazed on much of this territory. We keep taking frequent compass bearings and blaze a trail by marking trees with ax blazes and tying bits of red cloth on the crowns of the bush. Back of us a plane-table party follows and formulates a traverse map with station elevations over our blazed trail. Often it is necessary to temporarily change course to dodge the dreaded muskeg, a steep grade, a cliff or a ravine. We are really working on the first stage of the Alaska Highway now.*

*The snow is still about 18" deep in the woods, making the going very difficult on foot. Fellows on reconnaissance are fortunate, because we have snowshoes. We look like real north country explorers as our little party skims along over the deep snow blazing the way through the wilderness. After a day or two, a fellow gets the knack of snowshoeing and can make pretty fair time. We have been taking advantage of the long, light evenings and stay in the woods until about 8 p.m. Then we head by compass to the trail and locate our suburban, usually arriving back at camp between 10 and 11 at night. We don't have any trouble falling asleep after trekking through the woods all day.*

*We take a big round loaf of bread, a chunk of cheese, luncheon meat, and a few cans of fruit along for our noonday meal. Hungry as bears, a spot is picked under a spruce that has the surrounding ground covered with dried needles. With a beautiful vista on the distant horizon, we light a fire, make up our sandwiches, and toast them on a crotched stick. How good GI grub tastes out in the open! We haven't seen any big game yet, but occasionally cross fresh moose tracks in the snow. I imagine they hear us coming and start hightailing it away. Gosh, a moose has a big stride. I believe the bears are still in hibernation, because only one fellow found a fresh track and a bed in the snow in the woods so far. There must be a lot of bears for so many of the trees have claw marks on their trunks. No deer, elk, caribou, or wolf signs have been observed. Big white rabbits and a species of large red, striped squirrels are quite plentiful.*

*Although it was 5 below again when we got up a few mornings ago, the last few days have been just beautiful at it is warming nicely. Today the snow melted a bit in the woods, and it is quite muddy around our camp area. I believe winter is pretty well over up here now, even though the rivers are still ice-bound. In the marsh areas I noticed quite a few pussy willow bushes in bloom. Venturing farther out each day, I wouldn't doubt if some of us were to go out and establish a small camp nearer our work.*

*The nightly Aurora Borealis displays are still so beautiful and mysterious. Some nights every color of the rainbow flashes across the northern heavens.*

*The equipment has crawled its long way up into these forests from the railhead at Dawson Creek. Giant "cats," power shovels, cranes, ground skimmers, bulldozers, and all types of trucks are here waiting for the word go. Some of the massive road building equipment has tires 6 feet in diameter. You should see one of the giant diesel "cats" cut a path through these forests. Nothing in their way stops them. Tall, sturdy aspens and spruce snap like toothpicks and crash to the ground with a whistling sound like a snapped buggy whip before their power. It is almost incredible. After 3 "cats" pass through a wooded area crashing timber, the second clearing and the third grading, a fair road already exists in their path.*

*On a newly made road we take going out to our work, the "cats" went thru some muskeg in a low, flat plain between two mountain ridges. The ground composing of a muskeg area is like peat moss - a spongy layer of decayed vegetation many feet deep. During the summer it is always moist and water keeps oozing up thru it. Any heavy equipment passing over soggy muskeg either "hangs up" or buries itself, hence it is the dread of the northwoods road construction men. The countless square miles of muskeg up in this province accounts for the pesky mosquitoes and bothersome flies each summer.*

*Harry Spiegel*

One cold night we bid farewell to about half of the men who left camp for Fort Nelson, some two hundred and fifty miles away, on one of the roughest trips ever recorded. The thermometer registered thirty-nine degrees below zero; five carry-alls, four trucks and two jeeps set out over a rough tote trail north ward, through snow and ice, towards their objective. Some of the most adverse driving conditions were encountered in this run that have never been duplicated before. In talking with some of the drivers it was learned that it was absolutely the hardest driving and roughest riding they had ever done.

All trucks and carry-alls came through without any accidents (not counting fences knocked over by Starkowicz and Basciano) and the only casualty was a badly frozen foot suffered by Goodman. He was immediately sent to Whitehorse to a hospital, and from there was eventually flown back to the States. However, the cold had been too severe and the ride too long, for an operation was necessary. The result of which was Goodman lost four toes off the right foot.

Unattributed, *"Of Maps and Men"*

## Extracts from Sid Navratil's Diaries

*Minus Thirty*

*March 23, 1942          Monday          Ft. Nelson B.C. Canada*
      *This morning, at approximately 11 o'clock AM, we arrived at Ft. Nelson, a sorry flock of soldiers. In an intense blizzard we loaded the trucks, and at 11 p.m. (Sat) we "pulled out." Thirty six hours in back of a GI truck in a temperature that went down to -30 degrees! The air now is dry and crisp, which makes it rather comfortable.*
      *There was only one casualty: frozen feet of a soldier who rode in the back of an open truck. He was rushed back to Dawson by an Army plane, and his toes may have to be amputated. As for the truck in which I rode, we were comfortable enough, wrapped up in our sleeping bags and comforters. We were delayed by a few minor accidents, one of which was a "close shaver": as we raced over the narrow, icy road, the truck hit a thick trunk of a birch, bending it and then releasing it with such a force that it tore through the canvas, missing our heads by inches. It stopped the truck on the spot. Of course, we were quite surprised after turning the flashlight on - the wood traveled the entire width of the truck, tearing a hole in the roof on the other side.*
      *I have no light and it is too dark to see. My fingers are numb, too.*

*March 24, 1942          Tuesday*

      *It was a truly beautiful day.  The brilliant sun cut the biting frost, causing the ground to steam. We all worked hard, too, chopping wood and clearing the campsite, and now, when one relaxes, he has that comfortable tired feeling.*
      *Our camp has a very good location, it is situated high on top of a hill, overlooking the winding—now frozen—Muskwa River. The white aspen trees that cover the hillsides rise to a magnificent height, seventy or eighty feet at times. A motion picture cameraman took pictures of us in various degrees of activities.*

*March 26, 1942          Thursday*

      *Last night we all sat around the fire reading poetry. One can hardly imagine these hardy soldiers as lovers of verse, yet as soon as the "ice was broken," they all admitted that beautiful poetry was like music to them. To some of them it was a pleasure not uncommon to them, while others found it new and stimulating.*
      *Today we had our first "mail-call" since we came to the wilderness. A letter from Helen seemed to give me new strength and energy— which I shall soon need.*

Our new Fort Nelson "home."

*March 28, 1942*          *Saturday*

*I'm afraid life here is becoming monotonous again; every day we chop and stack wood. Today about thirty men from our camp at Ft. St. John came over. Tomorrow we may move to another campsite.*

*March 29, 1942*          *Sunday*

*The Sundays, it seems, are reserved for extra hard labor. We work harder and longer, grumbling at each ounce of labor. Today we cleared our new camp area, putting up tents, etc. My fingers are swollen from handling the axe, and the skin is dry and parched. We all are becoming accustomed to the horse labor, and morally we seem pretty well broken.*

*March 30, 1942*          *Monday*

*We moved to our new camp area today. The ground in our tent is all mud— but then, that has one advantage: we don't have to wipe our feet when we come in. Mac brought in pine needles, and now the interior is full of that aroma. Of course, we worked hard again, and I just dragged my feet all day long.*

*They say the captain is in the hospital; he had been working under a terrific mental strain. I took a spin in a Jeep, and think I'd like to buy one after the war; that is, if the government will sell, and if they are in decent condition - the latter being very unlikely.*

*The road to Ft. St. John is now unpassable; the weather has been extremely warm, causing the road to turn into deep slush. The snow is on the ground yet, and it's plenty deep. A month of this thaw will find us swimming in mud.*

*Sarge Ryan, my tentmate, is another man one is proud to have for a friend. He advanced from the rank of Corporal to that of a Staff Sergeant, yet it hasn't gone to his head. He's rather young—about 23—and acts like a school boy. I like to take orders from him, tho.*

*March 31, 1942*          *Tuesday*

*Chopped wood 'till every bone and muscle in the body aches.*

*April 1, 1942*          *Wednesday*

*Today was a pick-mattock as well as an axe; my fingers are stiff.*

*April 2, 1942*          *Thursday*

*Chopped...*

Never ending detail of cutting firewood.

*April 3, 1942*          *Friday*

*I'm a stoker for the bakery (regimental)—a job that relieves the drab monotony of wood chopping. Of course it means more wood chopping, but the pace is slower and there is plenty to eat all around.*

*It is close to 10 PM, and I'm sitting by the glowing oven fire. Overhead, the sky is studded with stars—there is no moon. To the south, a single ray of the Aurora Borealis reaches up high, rather still; every so often it disappears for few minutes and then reappears, very slowly, continuing its sentinel duty. The Polar Lights reach their full glory some time after midnight, and on a moonless night like this they appear to the best of their advantage.*

Fort Nelson, March 1942.
(Photo courtesy of George Behn)

US army pays Fort Nelson a visit.

# CHAPTER VI

## FORT ST. JOHN TO FORT NELSON CREWS
### TALES FROM THE SOUTH END OF THE HIGHWAY

### STARTING AT FORT ST. JOHN, WE HEAD NORTH

We were to survey "road location" for the highway along a great circle route between Edmonton, Alberta and Fairbanks, Alaska. This great circle route was already located generally by a series of small airports—Fort St. John, Fort Nelson, Watson Lake, and Whitehorse in Canada, and Fairbanks in Alaska.

First we showed the road builders where to put the road, and then where they had put it. Our work was only on the southern half, and we understood that another company did the same on the northern half.

About half of Company "A" went to Fort Nelson and the rest stayed at Fort St. John. Survey parties were sent out from both camps and ran into many problems. Maps were very sparse, and the field parties had many troubles over and above surviving the bitter cold. It was very slow going, and many box canyons forced the surveyors to backtrack and find a new way to the northwest. It could readily be seen that we could never get the road located in the year allotted to us, let alone built.

Meanwhile, the road builders with their construction machinery began pouring into the area. It was difficult to even use a compass, because we were almost west of the magnetic North Pole and the compass pointed to it instead of true north. Every few miles north meant a few more degrees that the compass was off.

It was decided that using aerial photos was our only hope. Even the most detailed maps of the area were so poor that we could not even instruct the Air Corps where to fly to take strips of photos for us. We needed a decent map to plot lines on.

The Air Corps made a series of flights about 50 miles wide, taking exploratory photos (both vertical and oblique) between Watson Lake and Dawson Creek.

Then we rented the St. John's dance hall, which had a large hardwood floor about the size of a tennis court. On the floor we drew the map grid enlarged to the approximate scale of the aerial photos. We added what few details were on the map.

We then laid the photos out on the floor, and were surprised at how well they tied in with each other and the sparse detail already drawn form the sketchy base map.

Now the real work began: drawing the details from the photos on the floor, using blue for drainage and red for man-made features. When there was a large

Drafting room - Camp Alcan.

distance between the photos taken vertically, we could pick up the same numbered oblique photo and sketch the drainage to meet the rivers of another strip of photos to the east or west, as the case might be.

We were given a week to do this, but it actually took two weeks and then three more days to pick up the image square by square on an overlay map placed over the original map mounted on a plane-table. This was done with colored pencils, and when everything was picked up, we had quite a complete map of our area from Fort St. John to Lower Post, which accurately showed the rivers that were picked up in the photographs.

This was the manuscript map for our first hand-drawn map of the area. It was drawn on English tracing cloth, and was a rather decent-looking map with names and adequate detail.

Black and white copies were made of this map and given to the Air Corps with the request for certain photo flights to be made, this time vertically.

When the piles of 9" x 9" photos came in, a key map was made with them showing their coverage plotted against the original base map which had been drawn on the dance floor.

By this time, several pre-fabricated buildings had been erected, and we were given a corner in one to plot the location of the road on the photos with red ink. We were also given stereoscope parallax bars. Starting at Charlie Lake, we drew red lines on the photos from one PI (point of insertion) to the next PI on one photo at a time.

First, several photos would be checked, using the stereoscope, to find the best location for the road, considering slope and other obstacles.

When it looked like a tangent line might be too steep, the parallax bar was used to determine the grade of the line between the two PI's. They wanted to keep the grade three percent or less, and that is what we aimed for.

Soon, the photos were coming in regularly, and the center line of the road was inked, and sent on to the survey teams which were working just ahead of the bulldozers that were knocking down trees, putting in culverts and grading a rough road through the wilderness.

The survey men in the field would locate their position on a photo, and

Tiddens Plots the map.

using a protractor, check the angle to the next PI. They would then tie red and white ribbons to the trees that marked the center line of the road. Right behind them came the construction engineers.

This process speeded up the job so much that before November the Alcan Highway North met the Southern Section from Fort St. John at Contact Creek—South of Lower Post

As soon as we plotted the road on the photos, and the road was under way, we started survey teams up the highway to run what was called a 3rd order transit-traverse over the center line to locate it according to longitude and latitude. This seemed like an unending task.

The surveyors would send in their log books of angles, distances and elevations, which then would be transformed into latitude and longitude. As the figures for each five-mile segment of the road were completed, they were sent to the drafting tent. We made maps of the highway with each map indicating five miles of the road location, plus a profile of the road at the bottom of the map.

We didn't know what a "conic projection" was when we started making maps, but were given a book on projections with instructions and tables. We also were provided with English tracing cloth, several sets of drafting tools and a quart of india ink. When the longitude and latitude were determined for a five-mile section of the road, we would lay out a conic projection covering that area. Thus, the Alcan was drawn five miles at a time covering the area from Fort St. John to Watson Lake.

We had to take the ink to bed with us, or it would freeze and be ruined. Six sets of drafting tools were worn out, as were several "Leroy" drawing sets. In the summer, dust would sift into the tent, making it necessary to keep brushing it off the tracing cloth map being drawn. The dust wore down the drafting pens and Leroy set points as if we were drawing on sandpaper.

Paul Tiddens

The remainder of Company "A," moved camp to Fort St. John. We set up camp next to the 58th Medical Detachment, who had arrived in the interim, and so began the nucleus of what is now Camp Alcan.

Camp Alcan.

On one of the details we stumbled on to a general store at Charlie Lake, about five miles from the camp. It was owned by the Somman family, and they became the 648th's staunchest friends. Mom Somman gave the boys all the milk and cookies they wanted, and would not take any payment in return.

Charlie Lake General Store.

After three weeks of general service activities around Camp Alcan, a ten man party taking a minimum of personal equipment, as well as a trailer loaded with transits, surveyors' compasses, axes, machetes, signal cloth, field kitchen equipment and rations, set out on April 1st for what was to be a 15-day reconnaissance trip starting at Charlie Lake. The first twenty miles of gently rolling land covered with young poplar trees was easily covered; however a chinook thawed the frozen ground, and the tractor-trailer method of transporting supplies had to be abandoned in favor of the pack horse.

The method of locating center line with the transit proved accurate, but too slow, as the 341st Eng. Regiment was following close on the reconnaissance party's heels with their heavy equipment, clearing a 75 to 100 foot path based on the blazed center line. The surveyor's compass was substituted for the transit, and location moved on at a faster pace. About this time the first aerial photographs arrived, and with the center line plotted on them it was easy to determine azimuths; and with the aid of a prismatic compass the advance reconnaissance party was able to keep well ahead of the clearing crew.

The 15-day trip turned into 140 days, for on August 18th the reconnaissance party reached the Muskwa River, where the northern half of the road started.

Havins Alsup Bollini Ulatowski McCormack Deem Vuilleumier Wilson Basciano Brown Lobaugh

After resting for three days, the men were transported back to Fort St. John by airplane, covering in 1½ hours what had taken them four and one-half months to cover on foot.

On July 5th, 1942, a transit traverse party of thirty men under Sgt. Teeter set out from Charlie Lake to run a traverse and level line over the road to Fort Nelson. Covering a minimum of five miles a day, these men, looping their level lines each mile and turning as high as 42 angles with a transit in a day's work, followed closely on the men grading and leveling the rough trail made by the cats, which followed the center-line established by the advance party. This survey, which covered the 256 miles of road to Fort Nelson, was completed in 88 days. From the notes sent back to the detachment at Fort Alcan, five-mile plan profile sheets of the road were computed, drawn and sent to the Chief of Engineers, U.S. Army, Washington, D.C., through Southern Sector Headquarters.

Unattributed, *"Of Maps and Men"*

## A RECON PARTY... Our Commander explains

The surveying techniques utilized by Eschbach's units were worth noting. In the arctic, the bush is thick. Visually one cannot determine the topography. The recon around would climb trees to select the best magnetic bearing on what would appear as the best general route. They used a Brunton compass as a survey instrument and a sapling pine as a staff. One man would set up with his compass on the staff and utilizing the chosen bearing, locate a second man, who would proceed through the brush, waving a signal flag from the top his staff as far as he could be seen. At that point, he would stick his staff in the ground, set up his compass, align it on the chosen bearing and a third man would then move ahead of him in a similar manner while the first man would then move ahead of him in a similar manner serving as instrument men or leap-frogging in this manner, the unit could make as much as eight or ten miles on a good day.

Alfred M. Eschbach

## THE COLONEL AND THE FIREWOOD

There was a bird-colonel; I think his name was Lane. Every once in a while, he drove his jeep as far as he could, and walked to where we were camped for the night. He would eat supper with us, and in the morning, breakfast, which about seven days a week was hotcakes. One morning after all the others had left to survey and mark trail, Colonel Lane said to me, "Corporal, go lie down and rest. I'll cut some firewood for you."

"Sir?" I said, and he repeated his offer. I took a nap, and the colonel cut firewood for me.

Later that day he went back to his jeep, but said he'd be back again, because he liked my hotcakes. This is a true story. It isn't very often that a colonel would do manual labor for a corporal.

Joseph Wyhs

# REMEMBERING

As the company clerk I was armed up there. I carried the payroll and had been issued a .45 revolver. I never had to use it the whole time except once. Everyone, with just rations to eat, was dying for some fresh meat. I was walking not too far from camp with a fellow named Warlikowski, and he saw a big bird under a bush, and said "Shoot it, shoot it!" I aimed for the head, or other wise the .45 would have

John Fisher and friends examine trappers cabin.

blown it to smithereens. I fired, it dropped like a stone, and when we went over to examine it, there wasn't a scratch on it-I had grazed the head. Faster than the wind, Warlikowski twisted its head off and gutted it, and we had grouse for dinner.

One part of the Alcan Highway has a slight curve in it, a slight diversion. The story goes that there was an old trapper that lived out there who offered the men a bottle of scotch if they would bring the road a little closer to his cabin—and they did! Ha!

I was asleep one night in my tent with First Sergeant Kuppe when something woke me up, and I was turned over, I saw a hole in the tent as big as a quarter, ringed with fire. I lay there a moment, watching the hole grow to the size of a frying pan, when it dawned on me that the tent was on fire, and I yelled at Kuppe to get out. I still don't know what woke me up, but evidently an ember from the stove had ignited the canvas.

More than anything, I remember the cold—cold such as I never thought existed even after winters in the Texas Panhandle and Colorado. I can remember laying there and actually feeling the cold come down on me. We did sponge bathe parts of our bodies from time to time when hot water was brought in to the tent, but there was no way to keep clean in the cold. As it says in the poem, it is true that your eyelashes would freeze in the cold.

Lt. Lancaster sent off for a book of poetry by Robert Service, and the men would console each other by quoting from "The Cremation of Sam McGee."

John Fisher

Sgt. John Fisher - laundry detail.

Highway surveying crew.

## HIGHWAY SURVEYING—A CRASH COURSE

The location and operation of the Alcan Highway required a series of surveys, each more accurate and detailed than the preceding one.

Crew 1 - Preliminary reconnaissance: This was carried out by a small crew, usually a Lieutenant and two enlisted men. Their mission was to find a feasible route.

Crew 2 - Road location crew: A party of approximately 10 men whose mission was to locate and mark, by blazing trees, the approximate centre line for the road construction.

Crew 3 - After the construction crews had cleared a swath for the roadway a preliminary road, a third survey was run, defining the center line of a future roadway, paying special attention to curve alignment and drainage requirements.

Crew 4 - Following construction of the finished roadway, a mapping survey was run so the actual roadway to eventually be plotted on standard topographical maps, geodetic observations were made for the latitude and longitude of major control points along the route.

Alfred M. Eschbach

The end of a day for a survey crew.

## PACK-HORSE OPERATORS JOIN THE MISSION

By mid-March soldiers, machinery, and supplies began to arrive at Dawson Creek the end of steel. Engineers commenced to travel up the trail toward Fort Nelson. Astonishing road building developments followed in rapid succession. A highway survey between Dawson Creek and Fort St. John was completed for the purpose of improving the existing road to accommodate the anticipated heavy traffic. Word went through the northland by 'moccasin telegraph' calling all pack-horse train operators (packers) into action. From the hills and valleys came Napoleons Calahoos, Callisons, Beattons, Belcourts, Letendres, Campbells and Camerons, along with Cree and Beaver Indians and a total of about 400 horses. The age of the packers had suddenly returned to the northland.

Don W. Thomson, "Men and Meridians"

## ON THE TRAIL

Late in the spring of 1942, a team consisting of Lt. Charles N. Nesom, John Shubert of the Public Roads Administration and me, with Duncan Beaton and Ronald McCloud, our Canadian packhorse owners, left for Fort St. John. We journeyed past Charlie Lake towards Montney and managed to reach the Becker farm before dark where the horses would be safe from the black bears common in the area.

From there we went on to locate the Bedaux trail traveling along a ridge which twisted and turned in many direction camped on the ridge several nights. With the help of trappers, we made it over the ridge, through flooded lowlands and across a river to higher ground.

At first evidence of muskeg, the mosquitoes attacked in force. The packers built smudge fires to protect the horses and us from the onslaught.

Overlooking Prophet River.

During these three weeks we had several rainstorms, some which left us stranded until the water receded. Whenever possible we kept moving and covered the entire ridge coming eventually to a rolling hilly area with many streams which made it difficult to make much progress. We reached Pine River, a clear, cold stream rising from a distant mountain which from our camp resembled a steamboat and came to be known as "The Steamboat."

We made camp on a large expanse of low brush and grass called Horse Valley. After several more camps, Lt. Nesom became very ill. Duncan Beaton called a halt to our journey. Beaton put Lt. Nesom aboard a good and gentle horse and headed for Fort St. John. I never saw the lieutenant again. I was told he was sent to a hospital in Minnesota. Without a leader we then began to retrace our tracks to Fort St. John. On the backward trail we met the bulldozers of the 341st Engineer Regiment. The cleared route made traveling so much easier. We could go as far in one day as we had previously in three to ten days by packing.

We soon set out on the survey for the Alcan Highway. We had one transit party and our theodolite party, three level crews and one taping crew. The southern part of the Alcan road was taped with a 100 foot steel tape, over taping bucks with thermometers on each end of the tape. Spring scales were used each 100 feet for tension on the tape line. The thermometer was read out, and the grade was read by both the rear and front buck operators. We worked our survey to Echo Lake.

Ira Kemp

Reagan's surveying crew makes camp for the day.

# CHAPTER VII

# FORT NELSON TO MUNCHO LAKE

## WHERE DO YOU PUT A ROAD?

When we arrived in Fort Nelson, we had a meeting between the officers and NCO's on where the Alaska Highway should go. One of the lieutenants insisted it should go north to Mahoney's Cabin. We couldn't figure it out, since Watson Lake and Alaska are a lot more west than north. We then decided to head west.

Mope - Conqueror of the Wilderness!

"By God, this compass is wrong! I Aint Lost!"

Cartoon by Cpl. Blackmon.

The first time we reconnoitered, there were four of us: Lester (Arky) Tolleson, Russell Smith, Vince Sullivan and myself. We went with packs on our backs and stayed for four days in zero weather. As we had traveled northwest, we ran into very large hills and canyons. No way a road could be built there.

The next time out, by way of Mike Quineandy's trapping cabin, was more of a success. He wasn't there at the time, but later, when the tractors came, he didn't know what the noise was, and when he saw the trees falling, it scared him very much. The tractors were the first powered vehicles in that part of the country.

The only map we have of the area had a Weasel City on the Kledo. The day we came to the Kledo River, a raft floated by with the Callison brothers on it. They were on their beaver hunt. They didn't think a road could be built in that country.

The next day the lieutenant had us build a raft to go down the Kledo. They loaded their packs on the raft and bid us bon voyage. The raft got as far as the first bend of the river and turned over. Fortunately, I decided to pack my bed, so I was about the only one to have a dry bed that night.

We made camp, and the next day walked to Weasel City. It was just one of the Callison's trapping cabins. They shot a beaver, so we had beaver and beans for supper. Beaver is good eating, tasting like lean pork.

Chris Gras

## Extracts from Sid Navratil's Diary

*April 7, 1942*          *Tuesday*

*Yesterday we finally began surveying again, doing plane-table traverse along the road from 35th Eng. camp. Today we began work on the actual "highway," mapping out the trail that was blazed by a crew just ahead of us. I'm doing the recording—and the beginning was kind'a tough.*

*The trail that was blazed ran through dense woods, mostly aspen. The snow was very deep, often coming up to our knees and sometimes, when straying into a drift, up to our waists. The road which brought us to our starting point had just been made by the "cats" (Caterpillar tractors) and was about the closest to a rolly-coaster that I've ever seen. We bounced up and down in the "carry-alls," our heads hitting the ceiling at every bump. We broke a spring on the ride, too, but the army mechanics will take care of that.*

*April 11, 1942*          *Saturday*

*Yesterday and today we chopped wood again. Of course that kind of work is meant as "rest" work, and tomorrow we will probably set off again on our plane-table traverse survey.*

*Wednesday we began working atop a ridge that is still uncharted. We walked thru deep snow in dense woods, and through muskeg, the latter being about the most desolate and wild-looking. Muskeg is very different from what I imagined it to be. The only tree that grows in it is spruce—very tall and rather "undernourished" looking. The ground is a series of bumps—I couldn't say for sure, though, as there were 12-14 inches of snow.*

Wood-chopping detail... again!

*April 13, 1942*          *Monday*

We had a day off yesterday—the first in about two months.

Chopping wood was on schedule again today, and it gives one a good chance to rest up. It seems that we don't appreciate a day of idleness anymore; it makes one lazy and sluggish. I wrote home for my camera—rather a new one, a cheaper one... Included a $10 bill for films, etc.

*April 16, 1942*          *Thursday*

Tuesday and Wednesday I went out with Mikezewski's party. We blazed a 70 ft. wide trail over the trail that we (Ryan's party) surveyed last week. The "cats" were only about a mile in back of us, tearing up the earth and smashing the giant trees as tho they were match-sticks.

Just received news that we're leaving tonite on about a 2 week trip. There's excitement ahead to be sure! Wild country full of wild life!

*April 18, 1942*

We moved out Thursday night and arrived at our new camp site little after midnight. The excitement of the ride was considerably lessened simply by the oft recurrence of such trips. The road, immense in width, was so deep-rutted that once, when I got out, the mud came to my knees. Yesterday we walked over a tractor trail in search of an abandoned provision trailer, hoping to find food. All day long we went hungry, having to go on a measly breakfast of three sausages, bread and jam.

All through the woods we could see signs of bears. They must have been huge fellows, as their claw marks reached well over six feet on the bark of the trees.

Of birds the grouse is the most popular with us hungry soldiers. It's an easy prey or mark for our sling shots, as it will not bother to move very much even though its feathers were ruffled by a stone. If it weren't for the fact that we're such bad shots, there wouldn't be many of them left in this part of the country.

Today—or rather this morning, as it is noon now—we have been waiting for a call to move out again. The entire ridge, on which the road had already been under progress, is no good and will have to be abandoned. And so we'll be practically starting from the beginning again, going to a ridge that is at least 50 miles from here

Just finished "chow"; one of the cooks must of spilled a can-full of pepper into the peas, 'cause they were hot! The meal wasn't so hot, tho.

*April 20, 1942*          *Monday*

Saturday night our party struck camp to return to our base, leaving me behind with one carry-all to await the return of a reconnaissance party. I slept in the truck—it wasn't a very comfortable night. Sunday morning I had all to myself, so I sketched a moose skull and antlers on a piece of cardboard.

*The party that straggled into the camp at 3 PM was quite done in, and very discouraged as their reconnaissance trail proved to be a false one. The road was abandoned, and begun over again about a mile south, on a (98th) trappers' trail. And so the Army roller rolls on...*

*At 7 last night we started for "home." The road was worst imaginable with ruts and great lakes and streams right through the middle of it. From one part of the road I had a good chance to observe the sunset over the Snow Caps. It was spectacular. The air was crystal clear, and the Rockies seemed very near. The colors were scaled blues to purples, and the sunset glowed orange.*

*April 24, 1942                    Friday*

*The tall firs and aspens sway gently in the breeze. In the gorge below me a spring runs on merrily, its water reflecting the brilliant sun of this day. It's spring now—grass and four-leaf clovers—and pussy willows. A squirrel chirps contentedly—the birds seem to flicker in excited flight. And, up above, long billowy clouds form designs in the heavens.*

*He is up there now, looking down upon this struggling, toiling, crazed world, happy to be freed at last...*

*Oh, Charlie, how I envy you your rest and peace! You were a true brother, and a fine man.*
[Sid had just learned that his older brother, Charles, had died April 9, 1942, of meningitis while serving with the Army.  Helen Navratil]

*April 26, 1942                    Sunday*

*We are working 16 hours a day, working like hell blazing a trail just ahead of the "cats." The days are long now; there is light at 4 AM, and at 9:30 PM we still can see easily enough to work. We have brought a minimum of supplies with us—so, when the ink from this pen runs out, I'll be without a pen.*

*Today we started as usual; got up at 5 and moved camp about 3 miles. At noon, we'll take over a transit line and continue working 'til dark.*

*The snow is almost all gone, and in its place mud is the king. It's lunch time now, so we're off again.*

*April 27, 1942                    Monday*

*This morning the schedule is the same again, except that we'll have to "lug" kitchen equipment as the "cat" broke down. This afternoon we'll do as we did yesterday: cut our way through dense jungle of dead willows to make way for the transit line. We're short a man, which makes it all tougher.*

*In the evening, Joe and I pitch a pup tent, spread our sleeping bags and drop off to sleep.*

*Not even the mosquitoes or bugs, or hard ground can keep us awake.*

*May 1, 1942*          *Friday*

*May Day—and our first day off. Great swarms of geese fly overhead, due north-west. One lone goose travels at top speed to catch up to the rest. Watson Lake is probably their destination.*

*And down here, in the beautiful sunshine, swarms of mosquitoes are making our lives miserable. They are much bigger than the ones at home, and their sting is very much felt. They work relentlessly 24 hours a day, robbing one of much leisured rest. Without them this country would be a paradise—with them, it is a veritable hell. So much for the pests...*

*Today we camped in the midst of a vast muskeg area. The trappers' trail is about half a mile south of here. We passed a cabin yesterday, and for us that was our first meeting with "civilian" life. Two Indian trappers were strapping packs on the backs of huge dogs. They were friendly towards us inquiring how we "liked" this place.*

*"It's just grand!!" we groaned, struggling to get out of our heavy packs.*

*Our surveying continues along the old trappers' trail. By now we managed to get about 4 miles ahead of the "cats"—and*

Mud... packs - are we having fun yet?

*that irks the 35th Eng's very much. We are getting rather close to the end of the area that has been approved, perhaps that will mean a few days' rest there. The transit was abandoned, and we use prismatic compasses only as they are less cumbersome and the work goes faster. I cut brush for a few days, and did recording yesterday and the day before.*

*We haven't got any mail lately—and our supplies of cigarettes and candy are almost exhausted*

*May 3, 1942          Sunday*

Chow line - Caldwell on the left.

*Yesterday our survey party came as far as Raspberry River. We came to a dead stop on the edge of a bank at least 500 ft. high. The river wound amid the tall firs and aspens, murmuring contentedly. Tomorrow we will move our camp to its bank, which will put us about 25 miles from the nearest Army camp, or 45 miles from our own base camp. Communications were halted by mud, so there is a shortage of everything.*

*May 4, 1942          Monday*

*We're camped on the bank of the river, and from the tent I can hear the rapid flow of the water. Our tractor crossed it safely with our supplies. Next few days promise to be quite easy as we're well ahead of the heavy equipment. A letter from Helen yesterday did me immeasurable good—few snatches of poetry that she quoted were just in the mood of the day.*

*May 5, 1942          Tuesday*

*The "cat" with our provisions hasn't returned yet, and we're almost completely out of food. God, I sure could use a hamburger a-la-Brass-Rail, with onions and mustard. The Army certainly has slipped up as far as food is concerned; they want a man-sized job done well, yet the stuff, and the quantity of the stuff they feed us is not worth mentioning. In the first place, our diet lacks any fruit whatsoever. For that reason we crave candy, and up here the PX is 25 miles away. And now, to add to our food troubles, the Lt. has clamped down on candy and cigarette orders, as they take up too much room in the trailer. One of the things we'll all get when we're back to civilization is a good 75 cent dinner—and real coffee with cream— and a pie! Hunger will sure make a man's thoughts go primitive...*

*May 10, 1942          Sunday*

*From Raspberry Creek we moved up 2-1/2 miles—only to find that we'll have to go back again as this end of the line is void. Yesterday and the day before we worked down Raspberry Creek to map out its course. It is undoubtedly the craziest river that I've ever seen as it changes its course at least 20 times in nine miles.*

*Friday Chuck and Joe were chased by a bear. Ryan saw if first as he was ahead, and as he ran past Joe, he said "Bear!" Joe said, "Bear? (pause) BEAR?"*

*and took off. He lost his machete in the flight, and it's a wonder he didn't throw his camera away too. They ran for well over a half an hour and the bear must have run at least as far, only he was running the other way. It was a big one, though, they said; it stood on its hind legs and grunted.*

*Wolves were heard again last night, but I, as usual, slept soundly and heard nothing. I may as well be in Pittsburgh as nothing ever happens to me.*

*May 11, 1942          Monday*

We all got up at 10 this morning in order to save a meal. The "brunch," which was composed of potato soup, eggs and coffee, was the last of our food stores. The "cat" hasn't come back and may not return for quite a while yet.

Tonight we did have one more meal; eggs (powdered) with cheese, some stew and string beans. That was the last of it, tho, and from now on we're on our own. We've been eating those eggs for so long that its disappearance has been a welcome one. What we crave is bread, fresh meat—and sweets. But—as yet there is no sign of the "cat."

*May 12, 1942          Tuesday*

Our provisions did arrive last night, and with it our pay day. Soldiers get their pay even tho they're in the trenches. I got a mild shellacking from the lieutenant because my notes weren't up to specifications. I don't think he knew that I had never before done any recordings for the transit. Next time I know they'll be up to par.

*May 13, 1942          Wednesday*

There isn't much paper to write on any more—We went back about 3 miles on the line today and started in a new direction—almost due South—to get around the muskeg areas here. An occasional shower during the day made our work rather miserable—and our walk back through floating muskeg made it even more so. Right now, in the evening, it's rather nice, with a bright fire burning in front of our pup-tent.

Well deserved rest after long day.

*May 25, 1942          Monday*

We're on the Kledo River today and the "cats" (de big ones) are again hot on our tail. The country is wilder, mosquitoes more numerous, and work tougher. The last is due partly to the fact that days are much longer—at 11 PM we can see easily. One night last week four of us got lost and had to spend the night in the woods. A solitary owl nearby kept up an incessant hooting which we did not appreciate. The bears are becoming big pests, looting our kitchen every so often. Bacon smell will attract them from miles away.

53

*June 3, 1942*          *Wednesday*

   *Billions of mosquitoes make this nature's paradise a living hell. We're entering truly big country now—giant spruce and poplar three feet in diameter. Today we're camped on an unnamed creek—some 10 miles from Kledo. The first 5 miles took us through desolate burnt timber and mosquito infested swamps. The days are long—too long.  Even now at 11 PM I am still writing by daylight, and after 3 AM, twilight lights up the sky.  More men have "gone in" with yellow jaundice - few are wandering through the woods, lost... God, how I'd hate to be alone in this wilderness. On some of these hills neither God nor man has set their eyes upon—and others have a beauty that I could never describe or paint.*
   *We're on the Steamboat Range, headed toward Tetsa River.  Well, I guess that's all—there's no more paper.*

Steamboat Mountain was a landmark whose silhouette
was forever etched into our memories.

*July 8, 1942*          *Wednesday*

   *Below, the Tetsa roars wildly; its waters break into as many as three channels at some points and then come together again to form a symphony of sound. Its rapids are wild, and it is there our fishermen find plentiful trout. The banks are either muddy earth-slides, or sheer rock cliffs on which only the mountain goat can find footing. And not far away is our first cold, white-peak, its never-melting snow and ice glittering in the sun.  We have reached our 85 mile mark here, of which about 35 miles were made during the last three weeks. The Army is determined to make Watson this year yet. Summit Lake, about 30 miles ahead, is our next goal, and at the rate we've been going, we should make it in two weeks. It's encouraging in that we had some months ago hoped to reach at least that point this year, and now we feel that the job may be completed yet. The Japanese attacks on Alaska (Dutch Harbor) may have something to do with it.*

*There was nothing unusual happening during the month that elapsed since my last entry. Quite a number of men returned to base camp because of illness, but others replaced them. Some of those have come back again (as today), refreshed, rested and cheerful. For me it's almost three months in the woods, and I'm one of a rather small group that haven't as yet "gone" in. There's Chuck Ryan, the husky Iowa boy who wears his Staff Sgt's. stripes on his heart. He seems to have plenty of reserve energy and will no doubt survive 'till Watson Lake. Joe Ludwick, my jolly tent-mate (I should have said slap-happy) is good for another 100 miles. Carl, a husky 200 lb Bronx boy will last forever, and as long as his humor is with him, we're all happy. The spearhead of his humor is "Trigger" Eschbach. Captain Eschbach, the man who has endeared himself to us with such comments as, quote, "Spare the horses; we can always get a man to replace another man, but not so with the nags." Unquote. Gripe, gripe, gripe; it goes on forever, but it is as much a part of the army as the uniform. Our food is still heading our gripe-list; we don't always realize how easy—what a vacation we're having in comparison to the boys who gave their lives in Bataan and Corridor. The only anxious glances we give the skies is when we're looking for storm clouds, in which case it is necessary to pitch tents over our mosquito bars. It's a soft life all right, and we will realize it only later, after we've gone away to fill in the gaps made by our buddies at the front.*

*July 10, 1942          Friday*

*Four miles of line run—along a sheer cliff on one side and crystal clear stream on the other—over mossy spruce forest and on sage-brush plains. An occasional shower between sunshines was enough to get our fatigues wet to the skin, increasing our discontentment. In pacing the distance, I was reprimanded several times for making my steps too long. The air was very clear whenever the sun shone through the clouds, and those crazy peaks struck me as ridiculous clothed in fluffy white panties. Last night the heavens were impressive in their heaviness, the clouds rolling heavily about the mountains' middles, the orange glow giving them kind of a stage-effect appearance.*

Laundry detail along Steamboat creek.
(Photo courtesy - Walter Church)

*Tomorrow we move again, and sometime next week—perhaps—we'll be at Summit Lake, our first milestone. I have a feeling the worst of our task is behind us now, and the going will be fast, if not altogether easy. There is one river to cross that has a bad reputation. It is the Toad, and one of the wranglers here predicts we'll lose at least one man in it.*

55

*July 13, 1942                                    Monday*

We are now five or six miles away from Lake Summit, and the 'going' is tough, if not for us, for the road. The centerline (℄) crossed Tetsa four times now and will cross it some more. There is a huge 5000' rock ahead of us called "Camel-back" because of its shape. On its top snow glistens in the hot mid-day sun; Carl and I want to climb one (a smaller one, maybe) as we did some days ago. We had gone up the "Tepee," an impressive 2000' rock of the Steamboat Range that could be seen even from Kledo. We had done some vertical climbing then, but it was worth it once we were on top. No mosquitos there; just a cool breeze that made us hold on to our hats. There was about an acre of flat rock on top — or rather series of giant boulders that cracked loose from the original rock. Somehow a patch of pines

Page from Sid Navratil's diary.

*July 17, 1942            Friday*

*We passed Summit Lake in a miserable drizzle. In the evening, when the rain stopped, the crystal clear water reflected the great rocks that towered above it. We camped overnight on the smaller of the two lakes, pitching our tents on very wet ground. Yet, in spite of a dampened spirit, I couldn't but gape at the weird spectacle of clouds just rolling over us. One half of the valley—a divide of two water-sheds— was misty, while through the other half we could see the mountains. There was snow in the gullies, and we realized that we were at an extremely high altitude. The following morning (yesterday) we "came down," a drop of 800 feet in 1-1/2 miles. Gradually the country opened up for us and at the very bottom, on a swift rocky creek, we could see the Rockies at their best. Immediately to our right were big pillars like the pylons of Egyptian temples. And to our left was the "Seat of God," a huge mountain of rock fashioned like a throne. It was so huge, and so close to us, that men looked like ants in comparison. Wild and rugged, its gullies hoarded glistening snow and ice. We came to a large creek whose bed was about a thousand feet wide, walled off on both sides by huge ridges. There were no mosquitoes there, as the continuous breeze and dry rocky ground kept them off. We camped there, and that evening we were treated to the most spectacular sunset that any of us had ever seen. Up to 9 o'clock, for about an hour, it had been raining, and the sun broke through the clouds just after it sank behind the high ridge in the west. The entire valley was engulfed in a red glow. In the east the "Seat of God" reflected the direct sun rays. The shadows were a deep purple.*

*Today we moved six more miles, deeper into the heart of the Rockies.*

*July 19, 1942          Sunday*

*A day off today gave us a chance to clean up a bit and to write those letters. We're on MacDonald Creek, some 5 or 6 miles from Racing River. The creek is deep and so cold it almost knocked my feet from under me when I crossed it. For chow we had fish; our pack train is long overdue and again we're completely out of food. At this camp we have reached the 125 mile part with about time as much as that to go before Sept. 15th when the horses will leave. I would guess we'll leave Dawson Creek on Oct. 15th; I hope that guess is good.*

*July 22, 1942          Wednesday*

*Two or three miles ahead is the Racing River and around the campfire tonight schemes were devised for crossing it. Someone will have to tow a rope to the other side, after which it'll be a cinch. The river is so swift its bed is in continuous motion—large boulders tumbling over each other.*
*Our terrific chow shortage is getting everyone grumpy. The daily menu: breakfast, three pancakes, thin farina, coffee; lunch (when there is any): two biscuits size of a quarter each (and just as hard); supper, fish and potatoes. To make the thing worse, a messenger who came to camp was telling us about caribou meat and pork chops that they're eating at the base camp. No cigarettes. Butts are passed around from mouth to mouth. Our center line no good half the way—the 35th are cracking down on everyone. No wonder the sunset and the country on the whole are unappealing. All we do is talk chow now. Very tired...*

*July 24, 1942*            *Friday*

    *We're on the Racing River today, and the river is one continuous waterfall in its noise. The MacDonald Indian tribe is camped on the other side, about a half mile from our camp. The scenery is even more rugged now, jagged peaks devoid of vegetation being on all sides. Directly across from us on the other side of the river is Mt. Mephistopheles (my own title). Last night, Spain and I stayed up late and the scenery by moonlight was grand! We heard same moose in the thicket, but couldn't see it. A night hawk kept circling over our heads, climbing slowly and then diving swiftly at an unseen prey then climbing again. To the west is a giant metropolis of rocks. (These aren't mountains but solid blocks of rock, the remains of the ice age.) After crossing the river we'll head for it.*

*July 27, 1942*            *Monday*

    *We're on the Toad. Crossed the Racing River on horses Saturday morning. The Indian tribe consisted of a silent patriarch of about 80 and a score of young-sters. Their skins were the color of old tarnished bronze. That day and the next we made fourteen miles reaching the "Valley of Silent Men" and the Toad yesterday. The river is very wide (500-600 feet) and very deep. It isn't very swift, which gives it a rather peaceful appearance. It's thick with trout, huge speckled 36 inchers that would go for a bare hook. Around us, barren hills and rocks. Our other party saw a she-grizzly with cubs—I never have such luck.*
    *The food shortage is acute, but we have fish of which I'm getting mighty tired. Oh, for pork-chops!*
    *No picnic this.*

*August 1, 1942*            *Saturday*

    *Moved about 12 miles up the trail, and are waiting for the 35th to pick a crossing. It rains almost every day now, the mosquitoes are gone and the work is tolerable. For chow tonight—ham! I'm getting to be a chow-hound.*
    *Time goes faster now for some reason. The days, too, are much shorter. It's*

Chow time for Nellie.

*after supper now. The tinkle of horsebells comes from every side of the camp. There isn't much food for them here, the ground being mostly either rocky or moss covered. Some of these horses are big, sturdy beasts, used to hard labor. Others are small and wiry, with protruding ribs showing. There is one tan mare with a colt—long skinny legs and big head, full of life.*

*"Sandy" and "Lucky" are the wranglers' two dogs. Trained for pack trains, they've been somewhat spoiled by too much petting.*

*Our next goal is Muncho Pass and Muncho Lake, and now that we've passed the half way mark bets are being made as to the distance that we'll have covered after reaching the Lower post. My guess is 325 miles, and I have a $1 bet on that. (It was 336 miles, so I didn't win. 1/4/43)*

August 2, 1942          Sunday

*This was one of those rare occasions when the "cats" caught up to our center line. The road looked good too; straight and dry. From there on, however, we took them over rocky slides with 80% side slopes—mile and half side hill (or rock) cutting. The boys all seem optimistic, saying the road should be finished by next month. During the last month they've made over 100 miles of road, but lately were slowed down by excessive rock.*

*Fifty more miles and we'll be in the clear, and from there on, it will be a matter of days.*

August 3, 1942          Monday

*Smoke has descended into the river valley giving the sun reddish glow. The strong gale is blowing it this way. At four this morning we moved out and crossed the Toad. A hasty raft and two paddles were all we needed to buck the swift current. I was on the second load and stayed on to bring the raft across for the third bunch. Nothing happened. It was Carl who stole the show, though, on the third*

River crossings... never boring.

*load. He can't swim and it was so arranged that he'd have to go back for the next bunch. He did well until he got into the rapid part of the river. His raft turned around and he barely made it down stream and then back to our shore empty-loaded of course. The camp is 7 miles from the one. The MacDonald Pass is to the left, and beyond is Muncho Lake, 15 to 17 miles from here.*

*Swarms of gnats greeted us when we descended to the marshy valley from—the ridge. They are much worse than mosquitoes. They're tiny and fast, attacking the eyes and ears.*

*August 6, 1942          Thursday          Morning on MacDonald Pass*

*A tiny lake that is cradled atop the high ridge, surrounded on two sides by giant pyramids in whose crevices snow is glittering. A strong wind is rippling the surface...*

*Yesterday we moved seven more miles to our present camp. The party ran three miles of line in the thickest swarms of gnats. Now a mosquito, in comparison, is a very tame and gentle insect. The gnat is tiny and squat, built for speed. In place of a stinger or proboscis, it has tiny mandibles with which it attacks and eats flesh. The result, a blood clot and a swelling. What makes them even worse is the fact that they seek concealment on the body. The ears are their favorite, and no amount of concealment will keep them out of there as they like to crawl under the clothing. One of the fellows had to strip completely, and there were five or six of them in his navel. His eyes were swollen and his ears were two bloody messes. Few more days of this and we'll go insane— they're impossible to bare.*

*For raw beauty, this country has no equal! Last night I watched the mirror*

Muncho Lake at last.

*surface of the lake. It was semi-dark but the tips of the rocks and the clouds reflected the reddish sun's rays. On the shore of the opposite side the horses were grazing...*

*After the gnats, the wranglers tell us, come the "no-see-um" flies, tiny, invisible insects. After them come the pis-ants, winged and vicious. And after those, forty below.*

*Evening... A swim in the lake—a vile chow (corned beef and cabbage)—last smoke before turning in. The "cats" caught up to our center line again today, making an amazing progress in the last two days. We'll have to "hustle" to keep ahead of them tomorrow. We should be at Muncho Lake by evening. The gnats were worse than ever on the line—everyone is full of sores from head to foot. Tomorrow our pack train goes for chow, which means mail from home.*

## 365 MILES ON THE LEVEL!

The men were selected to do the various jobs of surveying the road. They were divided into four crews: Transit, Level, Alidades and Taping. I was selected to run the level from Fort Nelson to Watson Lake. I had worked for the Missouri Highway Department before joining the army, so I had some knowledge of surveying.

When we were ready to start our work, we had to determine our elevation above sea level. Because no levels had ever been run in Fort Nelson, I took an elevation from the altimeter of an airplane at the small airport. They said the altimeter could be within 50 feet of the true elevation, so we started from there.

We had trouble at first because we were right behind the bulldozer, but we soon let him get ahead of us. All four crews stayed close together. I thought the taping crew worked the hardest and did an accurate job.

Campos, Frank, Smith and Balog on the level.

Some days we would cover two miles and some days four, depending on the terrain. Our crew level would set a railroad spike on a tree at the end of each day's work, and there we would start the next day.

I was told to run my line straight to Watson Lake with no check on my line. I tried to keep my backsight and foresight about even to compensate for any error in the instrument. I made a peg test on the level about every week to check for any error in the instrument. I used the same level all 365 miles. I wonder if any other level line has been run 365 miles without a tie-in point. We moved camp about every two weeks on up the road. We always balanced our level book after each page to see if we had made any mistakes in addition or subtraction. We always kept a smudge fire going to keep the mosquitoes away while we worked on our book. I wore gloves with the finger tips cut off so I could adjust the instrument. Otherwise the mosquitoes would eat us.

John Fisher

# HOTCAKES FOR BREAKFAST

Sgt. Price - our hero.

Sgt. Price could make a meal out of most anything. He is one of my heroes in the army, because he made lots of good meals for us. I can remember one time when we ran short of food and we had hot cakes, noon and night. I liked the syrup he had. I guess you could tell it "Price's Candy Syrup," because he would boil down hard candy-orange, strawberry, lemon, lime, etc., to make syrup.

It must have been kind of tough for some of the boys who lived in the city. We were busy the next few days cutting wood to keep us warm at night. I doubt it if some of the boys had ever used an axe or saw before, but they soon learned. It was just a little hard to wash or shave in the cold weather. It seemed like the razor just pulled the hair out. I'm sure we didn't keep out bodies too clean. We weren't G.I.s like we would have been in the States.

John A. Frank

# OLD WOMAN'S LAKE

A route through the mountain through a large valley looked so tempting with its ease of construction. I decided to take my Indian guide, Charlie MacDonald, and a string of horses to explore it thoroughly. We were on this reconnaissance from mid-July to mid-August. It was on this route that we came upon a beautiful lake about two miles long. I asked Charlie the name of the lake and he answered, "No Name Lake." Therefore, I named it Isabel, after my wife, and so designated it in my report. Charlie said he had also named a lake after his wife. When I asked him what he had named it, he replied "Old Woman's Lake."

One time when Charlie and I were going along the trail he remarked that if he had some squirrel hair he could tie a fish hook, and he might catch a grayling fish for dinner that night. Soon we spotted a squirrel scampering up a tree. I drew my .45 and shot it. Charlie was quite impressed by my marksman ship, so a bit further along the trail he remarked that if we could get a grouse for dinner it would be a real feast. As luck would have it, a grouse soon flew up and sat in a tree near us. Again I drew my .45, shot four times at the bird—and missed every time. Charlie, ever the diplomat, said very earnestly, "Pretty hard to hit him in the head." I would have been satisfied to hit him anywhere.

Alfred M. Eschbach

# TARGET PRACTICE

Along the Muskwa River, Capt. Eschbach rendezvoused with a reconnaissance party. A target practice using .45 sidearms ensued. The boys had difficulty hitting a twig hanging out over the water. The captain drew a bead on the twig and cut it off on the first try. He returned his weapon to its holster and never fired another round. The question Was it skill... or pure luck?

Chris Gras

Capt. Alfred M. Eschbach

# ALL ABOUT FOOD AND SHELTER

Warm rains and the advent of spring broke up the thick ice on the Muskwa River causing severe flooding. Ice chunks as large as a small room, and huge trees several feet in diameter floated down the river in a torrent of water. The river banks eroded, forcing the reconnaissance party to relocate camp three times. Seeking shelter from the steady rain, the men took advantage of the know-how of a local trapper. Bark was peeled in slabs from poplar trees and several shelters were built.

Chris Gras

GI "C" rations consisted of meat and beans, vegetable hash, G. Washington coffee and hard candy that made you thirsty as hell. Dan Dotta spoke with someone at the Bureau of Public Roads encampment regarding the procurement of fresh meat for "A" Company. Surplus fresh ham and beef arrived the next morning. Andy Coccia, an enlisted man, signed for the meat as "Captain Coccia." The next morning, a colonel arrived seeking "Captain Coccia," and hell broke loose. The meat was destined for another Company "A." What meat was left was returned.

Dan Dotta

Frequently on the trail melted snow was used for cooking or making coffee. There was usually a little competition among the guys to see whose canteen cup would boil first. Harry Spiegel was about to win, but he was disqualified. He had a floating rabbit turd in his cup!!

In the spring of the year Indians came out along the trail with their beaver pelts. They were without food and were eating tree bark for survival. The reconnaissance party shared their food with them.

The Indians thought the white men were "crazy" to attempt to build a highway through the wilderness.

Chris Gras

## CLOSE ENCOUNTERS WITH SOME NATIVES

When we got to the Muskwa, Archie Gairdner showed us how to peel an ever green tree and use its bark to make shelters. At this camp we found a wire cable from a wolf trap. We separated the wire strands and took the temper out of the wire in a fire. We made seven snares from the wire and set them out in the willows. The next morning, we had six rabbits, and while cleaning them, we caught the seventh. Harry Speigel asked how we were going to cook them, and we said we would cook them like kidneys: boil the piss out of them.

We proceeded up the Muskwa River to its confluence with the Tetsa. The Tetsa was running high. So we took out over a mountain. On descending again to the Tetsa, we came to Mill Camp, a trading cabin of the Quineandy's. Mill Camp was directly over Steamboat Mountain from Halfacre's camp on the Kledo River.

On the table in the cabin at Mill camp there was a note from Mike Quineandy to his brother, Fred. It said, "Fred, I have gone to Lower Post to see Fanny Tom and have a good time." What a man will do for a little sex. Lower Post was about two hundred miles away.

The MacDonald family of Cree Indians was there, and they were out of food. The children were eating the bark off the trees. We gave them some hard candy, and as we had a lot of dehydrated potatoes and some bacon grease we made potato patties and fed them until it came out of their ears. The family included old man MacDonald, who had helped pack into the Klondike in 1898. He took the name MacDonald from a Scotch prospector up there.

There was also Charlie, his son, Nellie, Charlie's Squaw and their four or five children, one of whom was a baby about a year old. They all wanted cigarettes, even the two and three year olds. Old man MacDonald said he wanted medicine as his knees were bad. Archie Gairdner said to ignore him. Because all he wanted was whiskey.

Charlie MacDonald's's father, Old Man MacDonald was always happy to see us.

The next day we went back down the Tetsa as the water has fallen a little. A few miles downstream we came upon eight or ten tents in an abandoned camp. Archie Gardner said that a whole tribe of Crees had died there from small pox. Old Man MacDonald was the only survivor, because he was at Lower Post at the time. The next day we arrived at our camp on the Muskwa. When the MacDonalds came by, all were walking except Charlie, who rode a horse and carried the baby. We asked Charlie why he didn't let Nellie ride the horse, and he replied that Nellie had no horse. Old Man MacDonald had walked about ten miles that day, so his weren't that bad.

The Kledo River camp was our next destination—back to where we were before. Some of the powers that be had been decided that gravel would be needed if a road was to be made, so we were sent to get a sample or two. Tolleson and Spiegel went directly up Steamboat Mountain, while Jennerjahn and I proceeded west up the Kledo as far up as we could go into a muskeg swamp. As we proceeded, we noticed the swamp drained north; the Kledo drained south. We were on the head waters of the Dunedin River.

Chris Gras

## THE VALLEY OF THE SILENT MEN

Our camp on the Dunedin was in a strange place. The cliffs on both sides formed what looked like human faces on the skyline. We called it The Valley of the Silent Men.

We got our rock samples and turned back to the camp on the Kledo. I got very confused, if not lost, in a rainstorm. Fortunately, Jennerjahn knew his directions, and we came out alright.

Our next objective was to get the road over Steamboat Mountain. Tolleson and Jennerjahn went west, and Spiegel and I went northwest. Two days later, on May 17, 1942, we ascended the highest part of Steamboat Mountain. Spiegel stayed up all night admiring the Canadian Rockies. When we returned to Kledo, Captain Stewart sent us up again on Steamboat Mountain to find a road location down to Mill Camp. Halfacre and his crew found a good location for the road up the mountain.

Chris Gras

## WE CATCH SOME BIG ONES

Before leaving the Kledo, we had to ask the Callisons if there were any fish in the river; it was the color of strong tea. They told us that the fish couldn't live in muskeg water. Jennerjahn had been trying to kill a grouse as we were getting pretty tired of "C" rations. Fred Quineandy came along and shot a grouse for us. While Jennerjahn was cleaning the grouse alongside the river, a fish came up and tried to get some of the entrails. Jennerjahn said, "The hell there ain't fish in the Kledo." We baited a hook and put on a rock sinker. The fish took after the sinker, so Jennerjahn put on a rock for bait. We caught five fish in five minutes, all of them different.

The crew then advanced along the Tetsa River, which was bounded by lots of muskeg. One morning we woke up to find Charlie MacDonald standing there. He had shot a moose, and had walked miles to repay us. Moose meat was a welcome change in our diet.

Shortly afterward, our supplies arrived, but there was no baking powder. For the next week we tried to make pancakes out of anything that would make the batter rise, including cocoa, but had no success. We ended up with chocolate pancakes and syrup make from powered hard candy.

The next day we came back to the Tetsa, and most of the crew went along the largest fork. I proceeded up the left fork for about six miles, and then returned to report that a road could not be built that way. I then followed the rest of the crew up to Summit Lake, the head of the Tetsa. We walked 18 miles that day.

When we arrived at MacDonald Creek, we went down it. At one camp on the creek our mail and supplies arrived. Tolleson opened his package, and began to swear and throw things up into the trees. His brother had sent him soap instead of tobacco snuff.

Chris Gras

Fishing for supper...

*[Editor's Note—The following passage is taken from Heath Twichell's "Northwest Epic:The Building of the Alaska Highway," page 126. Used with permission of the author, Heath Twichell—winner of the Allan Nevins Prize in American History.]*

## SUBMARINE SIGHTED

Despite setbacks and the continuing miseries inflicted by mosquitoes and "no-see-ums," most problems also had a lighter side. After a bulldozer crew under Lieutenant Mason (of the 35th Engineers) left their machine at the bottom of a deep cut during the same storm that sent the Kledo on a rampage, all that could be seen of the submerged vehicle the next day was the tip of it's verticle exhaust pipe. Although Col. Ingalls could chuckle over a radio message that said, "Send help. Enemy submarine sighted in Lake Mason," his appreciation of the joke may not have been apparent to the chagrined lieutenant. Nor was it in Ingall's make up or his mission to ease the pressure on his men as the day grew longer, warmer, and drier.

## TALES OF THE KLONDIKE
(The following is an account of a native of the area, Archie Gairdner)

Archie witnessed the last Indian uprising in Canada at Battleford. He was just a child when his mother hid him in the attic of their cabin as Riel burned most of Battleford and killed anyone with white blood. Archie was a quarter-breed.

Archie was on the Arctic Ocean when Vilhjalmur Stefansson explored Victoria Island and other Arctic islands. According to Archie, they once played poker, and Steffansson had him even with the board, but Archie came out alright.

Stefansson had discovered a band of "white-haired Eskimos" during his two-year sojourn in the Arctic. Apparently, these Eskimos could take a watch apart and put it back together so it would still run. The same with an outboard boat motor. One time Archie had a team of sled dogs on Great Bear Lake when a blizzard came up and he got completely lost. He turned the dogs loose to go their own way, and they got him out safely.

York boats were used before the highway was built. It took two years to bring supplies to Fort Nelson. Archie was on one trip where they floated down the Athabasca River to Lake Athabasca, then down the Slave River to Great Slave Lake, then down the MacKenzie to the mouth of the Liard, where they spent the winter. The next spring they rowed their boats up the Liard to the Nelson River, then up the river to Fort Nelson.

Archie told us an interesting story about the boat trip. It seems that on the first day, everyone's hands became blistered from rowing. That evening they built a fire and put in a willow stalk until it was all aglow. They then took the stalk out of the fire and everyone grabbed it with their hands until it cooled. The heat formed a leather-like coating on their hands, and after that, they had no problem with blisters.

Chris Gras

# CHAPTER VIII

# FORT NELSON TO MUNCHO LAKE
# HARRY'S LETTERS HOME

*April 11, 1942*　　　　　*Camp near Fort Nelson, B.C., Canada*

*Shortly after erecting this camp a few miles from the Indian trading settlement at Fort Nelson, we had a cold snap. It officially hit 37 degrees below zero one night, and a lot of frost bitten fingers and toes resulted. Just a few days ago it was 5 below when we got up. I have been out in the woods on a four-man reconnaissance party. From aerial surveys we are given a destination and from specified starting points head out with a prismatic compass with which to keep our bearing. What a beating and pounding the trucks take grinding over these trails. Some of them are warn out with only 5,000 miles on the odometer!*

*Although not in the heart of the Canadian Rockies yet, whenever on the crest of a small mountain on reconnaissance, we can plainly see their lofty, snow-capped peaks to the west. What a thrilling sight. On these treks we pass thru territory man has never seen. The last few days have been simply beautiful, and there is now a definite hint of spring in the air.*

*The snow is rapidly going in the woods, and soon I expect to hear a roar and crashing of ice as the rivers go out, once the expected Chinook blows in on a soft northwesterly wind. Most of us are glad to see the severe winter go, because it's not exactly a picnic to live outdoors in it 24 hours each day. In spite of the hardships, it sure is a great experience. The nightly displays of the Northern Lights are indescribable. What a phenomenon of nature! Up here the stars each night stand out like diamonds in the sky.*

*April 27, 1942*                               *In the wilderness about 40 miles*
                                               *from Fort Nelson, B.C., Canada*

*So many exciting and adventurous things have happened since our little forward reconnaissance party started out 2 weeks ago tomorrow, I could write a book relating them. It was still quite wintery up here a fortnight ago, as our group with its equipment and bed rolls loaded on two caterpillars started out thru the snow-covered forests, hills, and valleys. I was thrilled and felt quite happy to be one of the small group to be selected for the mission. In the swales and in the muskeg areas the going was difficult due to one and a half to two and a half feet of snow. It was pretty hard at times for our "cat" operators to maneuver their caterpillars thru the heavy timber. Once one tipped over on its side, and only with the aid of the second "cat" were we able to right it. In spite of the cold nights, with a good roaring log fire, a thick soft mat of spruce boughs to lay out our "fart sacks" on, and covered by our shelter canvases, we slept comfortably. After 5 days of reconnaissance, during which we gained much valuable information about this terrain, and found the route explored, presented excessive grade, poor*

*general bearing and bad areas of the dreaded muskeg for road location, we were recalled to the outpost camp. There we got a glimpse of the already cut "Alaska Highway" west of the Radio Range Station at Fort Nelson. The road thus far broken thru by the giant RD8 "cats" is a 60 foot wide, straight clearing thru the timber on the side of a ridge. Paralleling the road in the far distance, rise the mighty snow-capped crests of the Canadian Rockies! You should see the mud*

Forward recon party starting out.

*on the new road! It's ankle deep in places! I've never seen anything like it in my life. Trucks in the lowest gear are just able to grind their way thru the mire. Equipment sure takes a pounding up in these parts.*

*During the first 5-day reconnaissance and in the first three days of the second and present trip we ate nothing but "iron rations." As tired as we were of our monotonous menu, each mealtime, after a long, tiring trek thru the wilderness, the contents of those little ration cans proved quite hunger satisfying. The one meal we had at road camp was a real treat.*

*A Colonel and a few others took an aerial reconnaissance trip by plane over a large section of this area, and with some of their observations as a guide for a general azimuth and bearing, and some hint of the kind of terrain to be encountered, we started out under packs. Our party personnel has been cut to four now. Our second lieutenant has gone back too. Tech Sgt. Gras, formerly a surveyor for the land office up around Cody and Yellowstone is now our party chief. The second man is a lumberjack from Oregon. These two fellows are real woodsmen, and certainly are swell chaps and real comrades. One N.Y. City boy played out and went in, and was replaced a few days ago with a swell chap I have worked with before.*

*Two days ago a newcomer joined our little party. A Mr. Ambrose from the Bureau of Public Roads. He is a weather-beaten man about 55 that was up in these parts with a packhorse outfit a few years back. He seems to know his business. For quite a few miles our reconnaissance line parallels an Indian pack trail and trap line. We saw a number of trappers' cabins as we worked our way out here. They were deserted, but as traditional in these parts, the door was unbolted, the wood box was full, and some chow was on the shelf. Our Sgt. has a movie camera, and took some swell pictures of us nosing around these cabins, trekking along the trail, and at ease in our evening camps. Two nights ago we camped near a cabin where two Indian trappers live. We visited them and they invited us in. They sure have a nifty cabin. They speak surprisingly good English. Eight huskies sleepily lazed around the yard. The Indians use dog sleds on their trap lines in the winter, and have a few packhorses for transportation in the summer. On short trips with comparatively light burdens, small packs are tied on the backs of the dogs. I saw one Indian trapper come into his camp with his pack dogs. What an interesting sight! Spring has arrived here and the snow has almost disappeared, all the little streams are gurgling and bubbling on their merry way. The trappers are still doing a little trapping, because they can trap beaver until May 15th.*

*The Indians, whose cabin was near our camp had two beaver(still unskinned)hanging from the rafters of the porch, a big moose hide stretched on a huge frame and moose bones strewed the yard where the huskies had been munching and gnawing on them.*

*A few days ago I saw my first robin of the year. Aside from a few pesky mosquitoes, it's simply beautiful in these parts. Grouse are very plentiful. It is not uncommon to kill one by throwing a hand ax. Their mating season is on, and after one slides into his sleeping bag at night in the silence, you can hear a male grouse drumming and making love to his lady-love in the surrounding woods. Although signs are fresh and plentiful, we still haven't seen any big game so far.*

*The nightly displays of the Northern Lights are disappearing with the arrival of spring, but the moon and the stars shine down each night so beautifully on this quiet, peaceful country. Our days are already growing unusually long. It starts to get light about 4:30 AM and it isn't real dark until 10 PM.*

*May 2, 1942*　　　　　　　　　　*Beside a clear, cold, bubbling stream in the Wilderness about 40 miles northwest of Fort Nelson.*

*At present, our little group is far away from civilization taking it a bit easy around camp for a few days until we get further official orders to proceed with the probable road location. At this point one possible route to the northwest and another to the west exist, and with the aid of aerial photographs and recon by plane, soon expect a tip from the studies of the Army and the U.S. Bureau of Public Roads officials on which direction to proceed. After almost continuous day time going and daily covering many, many miles on foot since starting 3 weeks ago, this little period of relaxation and rest is quite welcome and rejuvenating.*

*Spring is really here, and hardly a trace of snow after a long, hard, cruel north woods winter remains. All is perfect, save for the mosquitoes. They are a real source of discomfort and a nuisance. It is amazing how soon after the cold weather departs, these big Canadian mosquitoes can hatch, grow and report to their battle stations ready to make everyone entering this wilderness miserable. The many large, wet, muskeg areas in this terrain are perfect, undisturbed insect hatcheries. They claim later on in the season there are punkies up here too. The Indians refer to them as "can't see 'im flies."*

*The weather is simply grand. The clear, warm days and the beautiful moon and starlit nights are perfect. There are beautiful birds in the woods now. Many I have never seen before. One bird up here is quite tame and bold. He is the Canadian Jay, also known as the Whiskey Jack or "Camp Robber." They always travel in pairs and are the size of a pigeon. Very bold, they get into the rations and fly over the pans when the cook is preparing a meal. Yesterday morning, just after getting up, a pretty male grouse, about the size of a bantam rooster, strutted in front of our heads about a yard away as we all lay in a row in our sleeping bags. He probably wondered what in tarnation he had discovered. He came back near our camp a little later in the day, and my sergeant took a picture of him with his movie camera. The squirrels are mating now, and they scold a lot, and do a lot of "fetzing." Just a few minutes ago, as I sat here beside a brook four squirrels in a row went racing past me hickety-click.*

*In the last two days I have beheld a sight, the likes of which I have never seen before—the mass migration of thousands of Canadian geese up to their summer haunts in the Yukon and Alaska territories. For two days, all day long honking V's of geese, high in the air and many hundreds strong, flew across the sky. There seemed no end to them. Sometimes a large group overhead would become disorganized for a spell. What honking and commotion as they milled aimlessly around until they once more were in for- mation and continued their long journey. I'll never forget the sight of all those migrating geese as long as I live. How wonderful and perfect nature is!*

*May 5, 1942*                                      *At our little camp in the wilderness on*
*the Raspberry River, B.C.*

*Now we are really getting out into this vast wilderness and far away from civilization. I am told out on the "road" where construction is in progress, the mud is so deep trucks cannot be used and often even the big RD "cats" get hung up in the mire. It must be an awful mess back there. I'm certainly glad I am up ahead in the woods. All our rations, supplies and mail are lugged up here from our base camp at Fort Nelson on the few big "cats" still able to get thru. Spring is really here now. The last few traces of snow and ice have disappeared, and the weather is perfect. It is 3 weeks today since we headed out, and except for a few snow flurries during the first week, haven't had any precipitation.*

The Alcan... where mud is king.

*Quite often we run across shed moose antlers in the woods and brush thickets. These moose up here sure must be big babies, because they certainly dropped some big "shovels." I haven't seen any on the hoof* yet, but very fresh moose, bear, and timber wolf signs are plentiful. This might sound like a tall one, but the night before last, the five of us were standing before our cheery log fire in front of our tent toasting our behinds, and in a moment of silence, in the pale moonlight over the soft swish of the nearby Raspberry River, came a long low eerie howl of a timber wolf. We listened and a wolf answered in another direction. Brother, that's really the call of the Wild! Even though we haven't any firearms with us, we weren't much afraid because these wolves have pretty good hunting now, and as a rule only attack a man when starving and desperate for food. Last night after sliding into our "fart sacks" we again heard a lone wolf howl.

We have a cook with us who hails from San Pedro, California. He is a comical chap, and in a very humorous way, is always talking like a Mexican. He has never been out in the woods before, and is easily scared. When hearing the wolves howl the first night, his eyes got as big as saucers, and he almost dropped a nugget in his tights. He moved his sleeping bag between the rest of ours and stoked up the fire until it was a big blaze. He's not too ambitious usually, but now a little before dark, without coaxing, grabs the ax and totes in a big pile of logs for the night fire. We holler "wolf, wolf," and he chops and drags in wood to beat hell. I have to laugh at him until my sides hurt.

One fellow is an Oregon Lumberjack and he, "Arky" Tolleson, also done some prospecting in his day. A real woodsman, last evening he baked a delicious batch of baking powder biscuits over the hot coals. Then before we hit the hay he whittled an ax handle out of a small birch log for a broken ax. He sure is a handy fellow!

The grouse up here are very tame. They have no fear of man. Last night we had two fried up for supper. One was killed with a slingshot and the other with a heaved rock.

May 6, 1942

The mosquitoes are still numerous and pestery. I'm beginning to get used to them, even though they are a nuisance. A couple of fellows are chewed up. Just after dark as we are about to slide into our sleeping bags on a thick mat of aspen boughs under our lean-to, the timber wolves begin to howl. What a lonely, eerie sound. The mosquitoes are still so pestery, but we have our nets now, so they are no longer a source of discomfort at night. Yesterday, an Indian trapper, whom we have come to know, came down the trail past our camp with three big huskies each carrying a pack on his back. He stopped to chat, and with a little persuasion had dinner with us. These Indian trappers up here are quite well educated, speak excellent English and are friendly. This trapper was headed for the Raspberry River where he was going to trap and hunt beaver. Each pack dog carries between 35 and 40 pounds of rations, furs, etc. One rather unfriendly brown dog had an ax strapped onto his pack, too, one of our boys who has a *movie camera took a few shots of the trapper and his dogs. The Indian has 2 pairs of moose-hide, beaded moccasins his wife had made up during the winter, with him. The lieutenant and the sergeant bought them. They paid $3.50 per pair.*

*May 24, 1942*                                        *Camp on the bank of the Kledo River*
*near the Steamboat Mountain Range*

*Our little forward reconnaissance group now has decreased thru a routine of "survival of the fittest" to a group of five, including a 2nd lieutenant, who is our Chief of Party. I am the only easterner left in the final party. The other four are from Montana, Wyoming, Oregon, and Texas. It seems most of the eastern boys "can't take it." Of late, in groups of two, we strike out into the unknown to scout the territory, over a period of five days or so without returning to camp. What experiences these scouting trips provide. Chris Gras, a Tech Sergeant who worked on mountainous surveys in Wyoming and Yellowstone in civilian life, and I are usually partners. The lieutenant said the principal reason we were teamed together is because we are the best long distance hikers in our party. We sure put on the miles in this job out here. Trudging thru almost endless miles of muskeg, thick brush and old fire-burned areas sure isn't a picnic, but certainly a great experience having its compensations.*

*Chatting with trappers is quite common now. From them we often gain valuable information about the lay of the land in the vicinities of their trap lines. The beaver season closed on May 15th. Two trappers came floating down the river about ten days ago on a log raft laden with unskinned beavers, some still in the jaws of the traps. They stopped, had chow with us, and chatted for a spell continuing on their way. We often construct a raft and use them on the rivers in our work, too. As one silently floats down a stream, it's then that big game is seen because it is taken by surprise. Quite a number of bear and small cubs have been seen in the last two weeks.*

*The longest two-man reconnaissance trip taken so far was from the Kledo River to Steamboat Mt., the highest one in the Steamboat range, which lies just east of the Rockies. Sgt. Gras and I went on that trip together. With full rucksacks on our backs, including five days rations and a stripped sleeping bag, we headed out. What a journey! After a day and a half we arrived at the first slopes of Steamboat Mountain. After a hard climb over boulders as big as boxcars, we began to ascend. Snow still lays in the crevices on the mountainside and often we sank waist deep. With every step climbed, the view became more impressive. Finally, after several hours of exertion, we reached the summit. What a view!*

*The snow-capped Canadian Rockies to the south and west lay before us like an open book. For a while we could actually see a snow storm sweep over the peaks. In every direction the view was incredible. The Testa River heading up towards Summit Pass thru the Rockies lay like a silver ribbon below us. Our road location is supposed to follow the general contour of the river valley. We had an exceptional view and drew several sketches depicting the surrounding terrain. I doubt if anyone had ever been up on that mountain before. We cut a pole on which we inscribed our names, the date, and "USA" and erected it in a monument composed of large boulders. We slept on the summit that night. What a unique camping spot! As the sun was setting so peacefully and gloriously behind the snowy mountains to the west, casting a pinkish hue over all the crystal peaks, I climbed up and sat on a high flat rock all alone on our mountain.*

*The only sounds heard were the wind occasionally whispering up the side of the mountain, moose honking a couple of miles away down in the valley, the clear, peaceful call of a bird far away in the evening twilight, and the occasional sound of a rock letting go and tumbling down the mountain side. How fortunate I am able to serve my country up in these peaceful settings!*

*June 1, 1942*                         *At a Camp on the Muskwa River*

*I sit here in the wilderness within earshot of the big, swift-running Muskwa River this beautiful June afternoon. The weather, at present, is neither uncomfortably cool nor warm.*

*Except for the cussed mosquitoes, it's perfect. Spring is really here in all its glory, too. During the last ten days all the buds on the trees popped, and this wilderness is now fully garbed in its summer best. Small patches of wild flowers are in bloom in the woods. Violets and blue bells so common in our nearby woods at home, glorify the forest carpets here, too. It certainly is nice, and the inspiration one gets from such a beautiful environment makes him feel good to be alive! All "Mother Nature's" creatures are living harmoniously together far from civilization, and at present, pairs of various northern birds, rabbits, squirrels, chipmunks, etc. are all raising their little families. At present we are many miles ahead of the survey party.*

*Now back to mosquitoes. They grow 'em by the millions up here, and, as there aren't many humans in these parts for them to sample, they sure are bloodthirsty devils, and at times prove most irksome and trying. At first there was only a couple of large mosquitoes to contend with, but within the last ten days a new, more prolific and persistent small mosquito has descended upon us.*

*Somehow they don't bother me too much, although when they are bad, I have to keep swinging my arms and swatting my head and neck almost continuously to keep from having my carcass hauled away altogether. At such times I wish I had a tail like a horse to swish about and ward off my annoyers. Nets erected over out sleeping bags are worth $10 a night. We have to duck under quickly when going to bed, so as not to let any of the darling little bed partners in with us. Then a whining, buzzing sound sets up around our nets as they try in vain to get in at us until far into the night.*

*At the campsite last night and the night before, a bat kept flying back and forth in front of the bed nets having a banquet feast on the oodles of mosquitoes buzzing and dancing before our nets. That bat is sure a friend. One of the boys in the survey outfit, whose blood reacts to mosquito bites, had his face and eyes swell up so badly his eyes closed almost shut for a few days and could barely see. He's all right now.*

*Now we are a real recon outfit, because three days ago the pack horses arrived! We have eight horses in our pack train. What pictures I could get with a movie camera now! An old trapper by the name of Archie Gairdner, who has lived up here all his life, is the wrangler and is in charge of the string. He wears home-made moose-hide beaded*  *moccasins, "kentucky-jean" pants, a big pair of lumberjack suspenders, an old patched plaid shirt, and an old weather-beaten slouch hat. A hank of gray hair always protrudes from under his old hat and half covers his eyes. He sports a half growth of stubbly gray whiskers and smokes a crooked, big-bowled, sweet-smelling pipe he keeps loaded with tobacco from a very colorful unique tobacco pouch studded with Indian beads. Archie is 62 years old, and even though quite thin and weather-beaten, he is as straight as a spruce and as nimble as a boy in his teens. Archie is half Scotch and half Indian and his wife is a full-blooded squaw. He certainly is an unusual character and a fine fellow. He detests anyone lazy.*

*Archie knows this country like a book and I'm sure his knowledge of this terrain is going to be very helpful for our work. I can't help but marvel at the way these pack horses can maneuver around in this brush, get over fallen trees and logs and thru tough places even though burdened with saddlebags. The saddle bags the horses carry are made of scraped moose hide sewed together with rawhide. They sure are tough and serviceable. You should see Archie throw a diamond hitch around a set of saddle bags on a horse, when shaping up the train to move ahead. He sure knows his hitches and how to pack an outfit.*

*Each horse has a different toned bell tied to his neck. What a pleasant sound as the outfit comes tinkling along a trail! It makes me think of Santa Claus and his reindeer and Christmas. The reason each horse is belled, is because each day when a suitable camp is reached, the packs and saddles are removed, the horses are tied until cooled, and after their front legs are hobbled, they're turned loose to graze. They are not grained, but head for the shores of any nearby stream, where nutritious, sweet "goose grass" grows. During a night's grazing, sometimes the horses wander a long way off from camp—hence the bells on their necks—so they will be more easily located in the morning. These pack horses are in good* shape, and quite gentle and willing. Archie is kind to them, and they in turn are faithful workers. Three of the horses have saddles. Already I have a couple of miles in the saddle to my credit. One buckskin mare is going to foal any day now. As is customary with mares about to have a colt, she keeps right on working. Archie said last night when the colt is born he will kill it and throw it in the river. That seems cruel, but I guess it's the only thing to do, because he can't be fussing around with a colt here in the brush. When that happens, I'll bet the faithful old buckskin mare will be broken-hearted.

We are now on what is know as the "Grand Lakes Trail." It is used only a few times a year by the MacDonald Indians living north of here to bring down their furs and hides to sell and to buy supplies at the Hudson Bay Company.

The trail is very difficult to follow at times. However, the blazed trees are a real help in locating it. According to Archie, who knows many of the McDonald Indians, we might meet them coming down this trail in a large pack outfit laden with their salable furs any day now. I hope we do, for that will be quite an experience. Archie speaks a number of Indian languages, French and English quite fluently, but as he says, "he lacks book learnin."

According to our superiors, the highway is progressing favorably. Soon our reconnaissance will take us up the Tetsa River, bordering and paralleling the Canadian Rockies and across them thru Summit Pass in the direction of Muncho Lake and the Liard River. Quite a number of cases of yellow jaundice have broken out in the 648th during the past few weeks.

Even one of our little recon party got it, and was sent in for treatment about a week ago. He started by feeling tired, lazy, and developed dysentery and an upset stomach. He had no appetite at all, and soon his skin, and especially his eyes, took on a greenish cast. They claim the "jaundice" is a digestive ailment; others claim the water causes it, but all agree it is not contagious.

Those boys who are sick are going to be flown to a field hospital in Fort St. John or maybe way back to Minneapolis in the States for treatment, it is rumored. It seems a particular kind of diet is the only way by which their condition can be remedied. None of the fellows out here have had a haircut in about 7 weeks! I sure look like a "bush-bauer." My hair has never been so long in all my life. I'm certainly on the fur-collar list. Long hair has one advantage though, it keeps the mosquitoes from stinging me on the neck.

June 7, 1942          Camp on "Great Lakes" Indian Trail along Muskwa

If the Japs should unexpectedly swarm thru this wilderness, I'm sure they would mistake us for hillbillies or mountaineers. Most of our regular soldier clothing is stored in barracks bags in some tents hundreds of miles away at Fort. St. John. Out here we wear leather hicut boots or, weather permitting, a regular pair of GI shoes, cotton socks (I bought 3 pairs of good *wool socks some time ago), denim overall pants and jumper (I have one set of blue and one set of the new GI green). Two weeks ago we were all issued a regular soldier's brimmed campaign hat. As usual, when I don it, I'm all hat, but I'm getting used to it, and it has proved just the right thing in the rain going through the bush. I have two suits of winter long-john under-wear. We will not be issued any summer underwear, I understand, but it is just as well, because wearing heavy underwear the mosquitoes aren't able to sting thru, and then too, when we get soaked to hide sometimes in the rain out in the bush, the "heavies" afford some comfort. We sure don't look very pretty in our outfits, but they are really practical. What little washing of clothes we have time for, is done by boiling the dirty clothes in a "dixie boiler" over a camp fire and then rinsing them out in a nearby stream.*

*June 8, 1942*                    *Camp on "Grand Lakes" Indian Trail*
                                  *along Muskwa River, B.C., Canada*

*This is another beautiful day. Large, fluffy white clouds are floating in the sky across a back-drop of pure deep blue. An invigorating breeze is blowing gently up from the Muskwa River only a stone's throw from camp, wafting the pleasant aroma of the many wild roses, which grow along the banks blooming in profusion.*

*For the last few days we have been held up at this little camp due to a snag encountered in the terrain a head for the prospective road route. Steep slides and cut banks along the river route and inaccessible grades encountered, if they consider crossing the mountain ridge, afford the problems. Aerial recon will probably, very shortly, solve the difficulty and inform us which of the alternative routes to proceed on. In the interim we are to have a few days of pleasant interlude.*

*A number of men in the field have been afflicted with "yellow jaundice." I had a touch of it, too, having about three bad days. Fortunately our little party was "standing by" for a few days, so it was an excellent opportunity to recuperate. First, I became slightly constipated and then lost my appetite. The mere sight of food was revolting. When I would eat a little something, it would seem to lay my chest like lead, and refused to digest. To "burp" was quite common. I became tired and felt so "logey" to move was an effort, and I just dragged around. With nothing else to do during those few days I slept and rested a good bit. The whites of my eyes turned yellowish. The ordinary victim of jaundice has his skin turn yellow, but I'm just too ruddy complicated, so I retained my healthy appearance. Urine turned orange in color, and defecation like that of a calf. For those three days I sure felt lousy. My eyes are just a little yellow yet, but aside from that, I'm A-1 again. I can eat like a bear. I guess I'm too blamed ornery to let some illness get me down.*

*I talked to two lieutenants about the jaundice the other day. They looked at me and said I'd gotten over it by myself. They assured me the* illness doesn't have any after effects, and said it was just an upset digestive and liver ailment. I'm glad it didn't get me down.

I don't know what is going to happen to our little advance recon party. One by one the fellows are dropping out because of illness. One sergeant was sent in about two weeks ago. He was the first case. They claim he has it pretty bad and was flown by plane back to a field hospital at Fort St. John.

Next, our lieutenant "just gave out" and couldn't continue any further. The captain is sending him to recuperate for a while. Now Sergeant Gras is lying up under the lean-to with jaundice. He's been pretty sick for five days, and doesn't seem to come out of it. He's losing weight and getting as yellow as gold. He just drags himself around. I feel sorry for Chris and try to fix things for him to eat, but food just doesn't interest him. Gras is a real friend. It was he and I that climbed and camped on Steamboat Mountain together. If he has to go in too, it will leave only the Oregon lumberjack and myself from the original party. I don't know if we are going to get replacements or what will happen to our little group. I sure hope Gras gets better soon, and we can continue work. One lieutenant said about 20% of the personnel of the construction regiment was on the sick list with jaundice.

*[Editors note—In later years, Sgt Chris Gras was plagued with liver ailments that contributed to his death in 1992. This was traced to hepatitis "C" resulting from yellow fever inoculations from spoiled batches of serum given to the troops. Sgt Gras's widow was awarded a small pension after his death.]*

Three days ago, the buckskin mare in our pack outfit had a dandy sorrel colt. It is a female and is lively and healthy. Mother and baby are doing fine. At first Archie was going to kill it, but then decided to let it live and give it a chance. That filly will make a fine horse some day. As I sit here writing, the eight horses and the colt are tied to trees twenty feet in front of me.

A few days ago I saw a most unusual and fascinating sight when the MacDonald family of Indians came down the trail past our camp. They are on their long, weary, annual journey from their hunting and trapping grounds to trade pelts for necessities at the Hudson Bay store at Fort Nelson. They didn't seem to have many loaded saddlebags on their horses, so I presume the catch wasn't too big during the winter. Archie says they have good trap lines up there, but don't really systematically work them. Sgt. Gras took some movies of them. They had about eight horses in their string, also a number of big dogs toting packs. "Old Man MacDonald" is an old, slightly bent and stooped Indian over 90 years old. He speaks a little English, and by using his fingers and hands to explain, can make you understand what he is trying to say quite well. Years and years ago he and his brother were the only two members of an Indian village not far from here that lived after a deadly disease swept thru their settlement one winter. He recalls the gold

The MacDonald family on the move...

*seekers up these trails during the Klondike days. Charlie, the father of the Indian family of eight, is a weather-beaten man about sixty-five. He speaks English surprisingly well. His children range in height just like a stair. The two men were friendly, shook hands and chatted. The squaw and the children stood in the background, said nothing and acted frightened, except for one plump-faced, black-haired little girl that would just kind of turn her head and smile broadly when I looked at her. I don't think it would take the little tyke long to get acquainted.*

*The Indians complained they had poor luck hunting and hadn't eaten in two days, so we gave them a little chow. What an existence they have. Only two of their horses had saddles, the rest were carrying packs. When leaving, the father and the oldest son got in the saddles, and the old man, the squaw and the children plodded on behind amongst the pack dogs. She was carrying a tiny baby in a big cloth sling over her back, too. The baby and those kids were bitten up by the mosquitoes pitifully. The little papoose's face was just a mass of red blotches from mosquito stings.*

*Shortly after they left us, the trail crossed a stream almost knee deep. The last we saw, the horses had crossed and the rest were wading through the water. Two little girls were helping their mother wade the current for she had almost fallen with her papoose. The father and the oldest son in the saddles were unmindful of her plight. From here they still have fifty miles to go before reaching Fort Nelson!*

*Was there anything in our newspapers about two officers and ten soldiers being drowned during May in a lake near Fort St. John? We were only able to get meager details on the affair. It seems a pontoon boat outfit* was ferrying equipment and supplies across Charlie Lake. They were using a pontoon ferry powered by a large outboard motor. We understand they had some heavy cats and road equipment on the ferry and the water was dangerously close to the gunrails, because they were over loaded. Either the load shifted or waves began to splash over the sides. Anyway, the pontoon filled quickly and the whole "shebang" went down like lead to the bottom of Charlie Lake. The water was so frigid the men never had a chance. It was really a regrettable catastrophe.

June 20, 1942          Saturday          B.C.

Tomorrow promises to be another big day. Our recon party plans on moving camp across the mountain range to a point on a pack trail on the Tetsa River. Four horses will be used to move equipment and supplies.

As strange as it may seem, I have never seen a bit of the highway being built behind us. They tell me the transformation of the terrain is almost incredible.

The going is getting tough now. We had a spell of real wet weather up here for about a week. Boy, it sure did rain. We were camped on the bank of the Muskwa River. Archie's eight horses and the colt always stayed on an island in the river where the food was plentiful. One night about dusk it started to rain, poured all night, and by morning the river had risen many feet. It was a "flash flood." It kept raining intermittently, and soon the river was a rushing, roaring torrent of water plunging its way from the mountains to the sea. I never saw so much floating driftwood in all my life! Archie's horses were trapped on the island. We feared they were all drowned. The poor critters were all wearing hobbles, too! For two days we watched them on the island from the shore. Then we heard a bell tinkle over the roar of the water and saw the buckskin mare come down to the water's edge for a moment. We were happy and assumed they were all safe. For a day and a half the bank kept caving away causing giant trees to crash into the water. Mighty spruce and aspen were helpless in the swirling current as they started their long drifting journey up to the Arctic Ocean. During the night the crashing of the trees would wake us up out of a sound sleep. About thirty feet of the bank caved away near our campsite.

After a few days the river receded some. In many places new channels had been cut and the course of the river had been somewhat altered. The next job was to get the horses off the island. The river flats were covered with a fresh boggy mud almost knee-deep. Two would float over to the island on a raft and two of us would catch the horses as they swam across the channel and tie them tightly to trees on the bank. Believe it or not, it took another two days to finally get our horses from the island. They would all start together, plunge in the channel and swim. Sometimes they would be almost across, and then the current would catch the little colt and sweep him downstream. Naturally, the mare would go to the rescue of *her colt. The mare was "in heat" again, so the stud swam after her and the whole shebang swam down stream and all would windup on the island again. Once, we had the stud and a few horses across and tied up the bugger tore loose and swam back to the island to the mare again. "Love is the greatest thing." Nuts!!!*

*Well, the colt had proven to be the real troublemaker, so Archie decided to kill it. He picked up a big club and swatted the little fellow on the head. He just stood there, blinked his eyes and whinnied. On the second attempt, the mare went for Archie. He put his shirt over her head so she wouldn't see what was going on. She wouldn't be fooled, and put up such a fuss Archie gave up the idea. The result is the mare and the colt are still down on the island. The other seven horses are back in the string "earning their salt."*

*The mosquitoes are terrific! I never saw anything like it. At night they whine and zoom around our mosquito nets constantly in a vain attempt to get at us. During the day they pester us continuously. A smudge fire is our only temporary relief. Out in the woods on recon when stopping for a rest we always light a quick fire and smudge it with green leaves or muskeg. We light as many as ten smudges during a day. I carry a head net in my pocket but never wear it, because it is too impractical in the bush. Even though my hair is growing over my ears and down under my collar, it is a real boon. The mosquitoes can't penetrate thru it, and I honestly believe I'm going to let it grow for the duration of the mosquito season.*

*Last week Sgt. Gras was taken in with a bad case of the jaundice. One of our lieutenants had to go in, too. They cure patients with a liberal dose of Epsom salts. Some of the first patients are returning cured. It is claimed there are many cases among civilians back in the States.*

*There is quite an article in Collier's magazine (May 30, 1942) about this job. There is a picture in the issue of my two buddies with whom I work on reconnaissance, Sergeant Jennerjahn at transit and Corporal Tolleson recording. The picture was posed, and in spite of the clothes and background was taken on a warm, spring day near our original base camp back at Ft. Nelson.*

*July 7, 1942*                *At Our Camp in the Mountains on the Tetsa River*

*I sit here on the banks of the Tetsa River. Thanks for the fishing equipment. I have had very little time for fishing, but did fish for about a half hour one evening last week before bedtime. I got two hard strikes on a Brown Hackle fly that really gave me quite a thrill. What a threshing that "fly" got when the fish hit it. On the second strike I could see the fish, as he leaped right out of the water. It was a Dolly Varden trout about a foot long. Too bad I couldn't hook him. If I have any spare time in the future, I'll wager I'll catch fish or know the reason why not!*

We stopped at a trapper's "home" cabin on the Tetsa River about 17 miles below where I am right now. Very few of the trappers stay in the "bush" during the summer months, so this cabin was deserted. He has a pretty nice lay-out. He even had a radio in his cabin, but the batteries were dead. Prowling among the trapper's belongings we

Barbering in the bush.

ran across barber shears and comb. Here was an opportunity! That evening with a stack of saddlebags for a barber's chair, we cut each other's "wool." Two different fellows worked on my "mop." They really did a good job. The cook is pretty clever with scissors, so he usually applied the finishing touch to our "nicked" craniums. Except for the mosquitoes stinging me on the neck and behind the ears now, it really is a relief to get rid of the long hair.

We haven't had any rain in many weeks and everything is pretty dry. One of our boys didn't extinguish a smudge fire he had lit for relief from the mosquitoes, and it started a good-sized fire. We managed to get it under control by beating it with our jackets after it had burned over a half-mile square.

Last night after supper it started thundering and lightning and soon a storm rolled down into the river valley. For five minutes it hailed so hard the ground was nearly covered, and then rained steadily until dawn. I thought my canvas tarp would be lacerated to shreds, but it proved waterproof. Tonight the air is snappy. This cool weather is a welcome relief from the previous hot spell.

We have feasted on fresh meat at least once a day. One night we were sitting around the campfire chatting after supper when one of our wranglers spotted a goat high on the rocks of a mountain on the other side of the river. He grabbed his 25-20 rifle, stole across the river and up through the brush. There were three sharp reports and the goat came tumbling down about 150 feet and landed in the bulrushes beside the river. The wrangler had fired three direct hits. The goat was a three year old and as fat as butter. He was all white and his black spike horns were about eight inches long. We skinned him out in a hurry and prepared for a big feed.

Two nights later we camped near a family of Indians. The father of the family shot a moose that day, and he gave us a whole quarter! All this fresh game sure is a real treat. It's got eating out of tin cans beat in a hundred different ways.

The Indians, although shy at first, become quite friendly. One evening we went over to their camp. All that moose meat was hanging on *poles tacks and low smudge fires were burning beneath it. This meat was being "jerked." The hide was stretched out to one side of their camp on a big frame, drying in preparation for being de-haired and tanned. A "meaty" smell permeated the air around their camp and flies were plentiful.*

*July 4th, I was in the saddle all day. I had to ride back to camp with some notes and sketches. When the day was over I knew it, because my "can" was a little sore.*

*July 11, 1942*                                            *Camp at Summit Lake, B.C., Canada*

*This is, without a ray of doubt, the most beautiful and the finest camping place we have had since starting on this so unusual venture last April. For over a week we have been working all the way up the Tetsa River. Progressing mile after mile we kept gaining elevation. The stream increased its tumbling and plunging over the rocks and boulders as we wormed our way up into the head waters high up here in the Rockies. All the while we ascended up from the valley, the mighty mountains, snow still laying in the crags and crevices on the side slopes, kept beckoning us onward. The closer we came, the greater their grandeur and beauty. This afternoon we hit the divide. Here, surrounded by towering, bare, solid rock mountains, whose peaks rise 2,000 feet above the divide, far above the timberline, is our little camp.*

*Summit Lake nestles at the base of these silent lonely peaks, reflecting a reprint on the crystal-clear, sparkling water. What a thrilling sight. I can see beauty in any direction from where I am now sitting at my "wicky." How I wish you could share this magnificent scenery. I have never experienced anything like it before! What an inspiration to live and enjoy the more simple, finer and more beautiful things in life.*

Summit Lake

This lake is about one and a half miles long and a half-mile wide. It lies like a jewel in these mountains. From the shore you can see schools of fish, about a foot long, swimming around. To our surprise, they are all suckers. Now that we are accustomed to trout and grayling, we wouldn't stoop so low as to cast a line in for suckers.

A few days ago, when camping back down on the river, three of us went fishing. We caught nine fish altogether. I accounted for two; and incidentally, the two caught were the largest of the catch. What a thrill, when they hit my fly! These swift water game fish pack a wallop that makes our blood tingle. I certainly enjoy this fishing.

Late this afternoon one of our wranglers took a hike along a mountain-side near camp for a few hours. He found a couple of natural "salt licks" and saw a number of caribou. So you can see, we really are up in the big game country of British Columbia. When I was thrilled reading the stories of this country in the outdoor magazines, little did I dream I would see all of this myself! Right at this campsite lays a huge set of spiral horns from a big horn sheep. Evidently a trapper or an Indian shot one on these slopes some time ago. Moose tracks are plentiful along the streambeds and in the brush as dog prints are around any tree back home in Ebenezer. Tramping through the brush everyday, we run across a number of sets

One of the local wranglers.

of old moose horns. Deer signs are also plentiful in this section. You should see the many ducks and ducklings on the rivers and the lake. They have a paradise here. Often we run across a hen partridge with her brood of chicks. A hen will always play possum, pretending she is crippled, flop in front of you and try to lead you away from her brood. If you get too close to the chicks, she will turn on you and hiss like an angry goose.

Last night I won a dollar on a friendly bet. My lieutenant and I got into a discussion about bears as we sat around our evening campfire. He said, "a grizzly was more black than brown." Having seen a few grizzlies a number of years ago at the Yellowstone feeding grounds, I took the opposite view. The lieutenant was so sure, he wanted to make a friendly bet, and I took him upon it. One of our wranglers, an old-timer up here, was consulted to decide who was right. Result—Lt. Lancaster bid good-bye to one Canadian dollar!

Most every day I have to do some sketching for our reports to the survey party following us. In civilian life my lieutenant worked for Federal Bureau of Public Roads. He has told me a number of times when the war *ends, I should look him up and he will get me a job for the Bureau drafting.*

*Now we are really up in the Canadian Rockies. The weather is ideal. The days are clean and comfortable, and the nights get quite snappy. There was a definite hint of frost in the air this morning when we arose at 6 AM. The mosquitoes are still with us, "bless their little hearts," but due to the cold nights, they work only the day shift.*

*Next week we expect to catch up with our Indian friends up ahead on Racing River. I have a pair of moose hide moccasins ordered from the squaw. They are just the thing to wear around the camp in the evenings.*

*July 16, 1942                                    A camp on the Toad River*

*We are moving steadily on the job now, in the center of the Rocky range. The scenery surely rivals that of Switzerland. I shall never forget this experience.*

*We had more fish than we could eat for supper last night; 36 trout and grayling. They were cleaned and in the pan less than an hour after being caught. Sure is great country! I saw a mountain sheep on a distant mountain this morning. A cow moose and a grizzly bear were seen yesterday.*

*The river we are camped on will be forded soon, and I'm afraid it will be quite a job because these streams up in this vicinity are big, deep, and "going places" in a hurry. The scenery is still so beautiful. I could go on for pages describing its grandeur. Towering mountains, deep valleys, rushing streams and sparkling lakes abound. How I wish you could share this most incredible scenery!*

*The other night a couple of us went fishing after supper. We caught a dandy mess of trout. I caught two, both about 16 inches long. We use a plain hook baited with a fish fin. Those trout sure made a delicious breakfast with flapjacks. I shall describe the food we eat. Since we have packhorses and are on a twenty-day ration system, our meals have improved a great deal. We have a steady cook, too. Naturally most of our food comes out of cans. Fresh meat is only to be had when some animal gets between the sights of our wrangler's rifle. Lately, luck has been poor. Breakfast consists of pancakes (sometimes with jam or jelly) canned butter, oatmeal or farina cereal and coffee. Occasionally we have canned sausages with our flapjacks. At noon we eat C-Rations. These get tiresome, but they are bearable once a day. We usually have a good supper. When the cook feels ambitious (which isn't too often) we have hot campfire biscuits. Canned meat consists of vegetable stew, corned beef, vienna sausage and mackerel or salmon. We get some bacon, but hams are scarce as hen's teeth. Canned vegetables consist of spinach, corn, tomatoes, peas, beets, and diced carrots. We don't get much canned fruit. What little we do get is either fruit cocktail, peaches, pears, or prunes. To supplement these canned foods we have quite a bit of dried and dehydrated items such as dried peaches,* apricots, raisins, potato shreds, cabbage, onion flakes, rice, and orange and lemon crystals for soft drinks. I should also list bouillon cubes, coffee, tea, cocoa and dehydrated milk.

All in all, under the conditions, we eat fairly well. Sometimes the diet gets monotonous, but we always get enough to eat. Lately we have been receiving some fruit juices. These are a special treat and were purchased here in Canada, by our Captain, out of the Company Fund.

July 23, 1942

I haven't seen any civilians since hitting the wilderness up here last spring. Except for an Indian squaw, haven't seen a woman since leaving Fort St. John in a bitter snowstorm last March. Many pleasant and many unpleasant, but all most interesting things have transpired since then. So far this has all been so adventurous and a great experience.

I understand the censors are now cutting our parts of my letters. I sincerely hope none of my letters will need censoring in the future, because I don't want to write about anything that might retard the progress of our job or be detrimental to the final victory in the War.

In connection with this, it recalls a little clipping I read a few days ago in a California newspaper one of the boys received. It seems a soldier engaged somewhere in the Pacific conflict wrote a long mushy letter to his girlfriend back in the States in which he also blabbed a lot of secret military information that would have been a juicy morsel for the enemy to hear. As it passed thru the mail channels, naturally the letter was censored. As the story goes, the censor became weary of striking out line after line of the lad's letter, so to save time he destroyed it, and sent the gal a note saying, "Your boyfriend still loves you, but he talks too much!"

Archie, the Scotch-Indian wrangler I wrote about is no longer with us. This might sound amusing, but he went in because his squaw is expecting a papoose any day. I judge Archie to be about 65 years old. Either this moose meat is mighty potent, or he has good neighbors! We don't expect him back with us. His string of horses is still out here, but is attached to the survey party. [Editor's note—Taking Archie's place was 19 year old Garnet Harrold, a bush smart and horse smart Indian from Fort Nelson.]

The mare and the little colt were finally rescued from the island. The mare was so wild after being on the island alone for so long she had to be snared before they could put a halter on her. The last time I was back to the survey camp with some recon sketches and notes I saw the mare and the colt. The little fellow is doing fine and it is a comical sight to see him following his Ma as the pack string moves along the trail. Our recon party has almost twenty horses in its string now. They make a pretty sight winding along the trails toting their packs. We have two swell wranglers, too. One is a young trapper and the other a homesteader from Alberta. Those men sure are interesting and a part of this wilderness country.

*The other day we crossed the Racing River at a ford with out pack outfit. No white man has ever penetrated to its headwaters, but it is believed the river originates at the base of a glacier, because the water is always a gray, milky color. It sure is well named, for that body of water is really moving. It was quite a thrill fording on horseback. The horses crossed the stream at a diagonal, water gushing up around their chests and their tails floating our straight in the wake left behind them. In places the horses were barely able to touch bottom.*

Pack-team crossing the Toad River.

*July 30, 1942*                    *Camp on Toad River, B.C., Canada*

*We are now in the heart of the second range of the Rockies. The higher mountains are bare rock and well above timberline. On cloudy days the higher peaks are obscured in swirling clouds, and on clear, bright days are a most impressive sight as they stand as lonely sentinels against a backdrop of deep blue sky reaching towards their Creator.*
*The river valley we are now working in is walled in by a range of mountains on either side. In many places bad rock slides come right down to the rushing, plunging river. Here the trail hangs on the slides just above the water's edge, and such places prove pretty risky to bring a pack outfit safely thru. A few days ago an outfit was passing along such a slide area just below our present camp when two of the horses slid off a big slanted rock into the river. They were toting packs as they hit the water, the current pulled them into the river and all were carried downstream. They began to swim, and finally landed on a gravel bar downstream on the opposite side of the river. It's surprising how well a horse can swim in fast water even when loaded with a heavy pack. At a time like this it is important to keep the rest of the string from getting excited and out of control. The two horses refused to come back on their own, so two of the trappers working for the party had to raft across and re-swim the packers back and get the outfit rolling once more. That mishap cost us almost half a day in time. There are always some unexpected, exciting experiences like this to spruce up our life out here in this lonely wilderness.*

I am getting to be quite a hand at making rafts. Two pieces of rope and an ax are all that are necessary for making a good one. I've even learned how to whittle a paddle from an aspen log. Indeed, "necessity is the mother of invention." We have to raft across streams quite often in order to reconnaissance on the opposite banks.

The days get quite warm in the afternoon, but each night, soon after supper, when the cool air blows down from the mountainsides, the warm glow from our campfire is most inviting and comfortable. It's really an ideal summer climate. During the last ten days the mosquitoes have practically disappeared. What a welcome relief from those pests! According to the wranglers with our party, we will get some relief from insects for a short spell now, and then come the "can't see 'me" flies. In early September there are supposed to be millions of them. They become so thick and hang around a person in a cloud. They are reported to be a continuous source of discomfort, even at night, and are so small they easily penetrate an ordinary mosquito net. I'm not looking forward to the little pests.

We have been busy, and have little leisure time for fishing. However, occasionally some of our meals are supplemented by fresh-caught trout. The hooks and fishing tackle from home have already proved their worth.

I can say little about our mission except it is progressing rapidly. Sgt. Gras and the Lieutenant are leaving in the morning for an extended recon trip ahead. I wish I could go along, as it promises to be a most interesting journey. Some reorganization is going to take place soon, and I expect to go out with a small party on an advance recon, too. Of course I am not able to mention destinations, distances, etc.

August 9, 1942          Sunday          Camped on the shore of a large lake
                                        [Editor's Note—Muncho Lake]


So many interesting and exciting events have taken place in the last ten days I hardly know where to begin. My experiences since I last wrote have been the most interesting.

To start with, I saw the remains of an old Indian colony down on the River. The MacDonalds lived happily there many years back on the banks on the banks of that river nestled between these beautiful towering mountains, until a terrible plague struck. When two of the braves returned from a distant hunting trip in the dead of the Arctic winter they found every soul in the village dead. One of these survivors is the Old Man MacDonald I described in my past writings. This tale accounts for the fact tribes no longer can exist up in this country. Only a few Indian families now represent the red men who once called this beautiful land their own.

At the old village site only rotted remains of their cabins remain. On the bank of the river was an old Indian grave. The mound of the grave was enclosed with a log fence about two and a half feet high. A rustic wooden cross was set up at the head of the grave.

The "no see'ems" are here en masse now. Those little brats are terrible! As bad as the mosquitoes were, we all agree these punkies are worse. There just isn't any way to escape them. They are supposed to get worse as fall approaches and stay 'til the first hard frost. Out in the bush they just buzz around a person's head in a cloud. One doesn't feel them bite or sting till they draw blood. Some of the boys have bloody necks, foreheads and ears. The gnats really take a chunk out when they bite causing a welt to swell. Our heads and necks are just a series of red welts that stay sore for a while. Washing frequently with a soap lather is soothing. Some of the        fellow's eyes are so swollen and puffed up they can hardly see. My eyes were swollen from the gnat bites when I got up this morning.  These blamed pests are able to work down into a fellow's clothes and sting him on the chest and around the waist. Fortunately, they retire at night and under our mosquito nets we can get a good night's sleep. The mosquitoes are all gone now, giving the "can't see'ems" a lot of territory to cover with no competition.

One of the boys received a very recent (July or August) copy of the Reader's Digest. In it an article entitled "Battlefront in the Wilderness" gives a very honest, fact-filled, interesting account of our job here since we arrived last spring. Our lieutenant received a radiogram from Staff Headquarters that two men who knew the country from advance reconnaissance were to go ahead with the necessary string of horses to the Lake and meet a Major, a Captain, and a civilian location engineer. Our job was to guide them up thru an Indian pass not then being considered as a possible route. Tolleson, my lumberjack friend, and I were picked for the mission. We picked out four day's chow for our trip, necessary pots and skillets, packed panniers the night before, and the next morning, after packing two pack horses and five saddle horses, Tolleson and I started out thru the divide for the Lake as our envious comrades looked on.  The colt came along, too, because his mother was one of the horses in our string. After a seven hour journey over a divide, we arrived at the beautiful lake. It is the largest one in this sector. We unpacked our horses, turned them out to graze and cooked ourselves a good supper. Tolleson and I had set up our tent and were toasting our shins before a campfire about dusk when we heard a plane approaching from around the mountain range. Our visitors were arriving! Soon a pretty yellow seaplane with metal pontoons skimmed over the horizon. The wing and tail lights were lit on the plane. We waved from the shore and stoked our campfire so the pilot could spot us. They circled once and sat the plane down on the lake just as pretty as a picture.

The plane taxied across to our camp and cut the motor. The lines were thrown from the pontoon floats and moored fast. We introduced ourselves and offered them the hospitality and meager comforts of our little camp. Tolleson and I set up their tent, made up a kettle of cocoa, and after a brief chat with our visitors, went to bed.

The next morning we got up early, made breakfast for our party, wrangled the horses, packed them, and started our trip in the saddle up into the Indian pass. The weather was perfect, and after a seven-hour up-hill climb following rocky creek beds arrived at the summit. The "seats" of our three guests were so sore they found it painful to stay in their saddles during the last few hours of the journey. What a grand spot we had to camp that night in the mountain pass. We made a good supper in jig time, which impressed our guests. They had never been on a pack outfit camping trip, so the experience was quite an event for them. As they watched us, the Major and the Captain asked what our occupations were in civilian life. The next morning, right after breakfast, we started down the canyon again with our outfit. We arrived at the original camp on the lake about suppertime that evening. Tolleson and I whipped up a good supper including bannock and all ate heartily. The Major and his party were grateful for anything we did for them and proved perfect partners. Now I feel I am able to qualify as a "dude" wrangler. It was really a pleasant experience, which shall be long remembered.

Harry Spiegel - "dude wrangler."

# CHAPTER IX

# MUNCHO TO CONTACT CREEK
# NORTH & SOUTH MEET

Ferrying equipment on pontoon barges past the cliff face at Muncho Lake.
(Photo courtesy - Walter Church - 35th Eng.)

**Extracts from Sid Navratil's Diaries**

*August 9, 1942*       *Monday*       *Muncho Lake [Aug 8-Sid's 26th birthday]*

*Friday night we reached the lake after fighting our way through thick swarms of gnats, and forests of spruce and jack-pine. The "cats" were on our tails and next morning, as we moved out, they were already ahead of us, beginning to blast their way along the ten mile lake shore. At noon, when we stopped for a swim and rest, we noticed a black column of smoke behind us in the vicinity of our old camp; few hours later, one entire ridge was aflame, sending clouds of smoke up to "red-out" the sun. As the wind was blowing strongly in our direction, we entertained ideas of building a raft, just in case we were stranded. A large coulee at about the half-way point on the lake halted the fire last night; whether the fire will spread, we won't know for sure yet.*

*August 12, 1942*        *Wednesday*        *On the Trout River*

Swift progress was made by our two parties the last three days. Today's camp is 22 miles west of Muncho Lake, in the...

*August 13, 1942*        *Thursday*

I fell asleep in the middle of the sentence yesterday...

We moved five more miles today. Camped again on the Trout, and we're without mosquito bars and tents. The sky is a cerulean blue and not an insect in sight. It must be the wind. I can't understand it. We are nearing the Liard, the Mother Volga of Canada.

*August 17, 1942*        *Sunday*        *On the Liard River*

Friday we camped on the River, and yesterday the center line was brought to its bank. That night we rafted across the swift stream. The river is about 200 yards wide, and 18 feet deep, and its current, even though not seeming to be fast, is so strong it took us 10 minutes to cross it. The horses had a hard time of it, snorting and fuming. The stud, the gray "Beast" and the little colt led the herd. The colt's entire neck and part of his body even were out of the water. The donkey did well, also, practically floating on top of the water. One of the grays went under several times and was almost swept away by the strong current the Trout makes when it empties into the Liard.

Today we worked over a wind-burn area, a treacherous stretch of rotten logs. Burn areas are our hardest, and this of all was the worst.
In two or three weeks we'll be at Lower Post—so we're told. Which shortens our schedule by a great deal.

*August 21, 1942*        *Friday*        *On the Liard*

We are approximately 15 miles up river from the crossing. The wind-burn is far behind us now, and the work goes on through big spruce and tall birch and aspen. We are not progressing as fast as we thought we would as the line we are locating now will be a permanent one, a 90-feet clearing that will remain as is, the Alcan Road. Still we should be finished by Sept. 15th.

A pack of wolves has been following our trail for days now. Their cries in the night are the weirdest sounds one can hear. Fresh bear tracks made over our own are every evidence they're near, yet we don't see them. The sunsets are grand in the evenings—a blaze of gold, and red, and purple. A great white eagle circling over our camp at dusk one evening made a wonderful shot for the camera fiends.

The horses are being packed now (it's morning) for another jump up the river. Every day now we're getting closer to the end—and closer to home.

Camp along the "Alcan."

*August 24, 1942          Monday          On the Liard*

*A twelve mile jump today, and another one tomorrow will put us some 50 miles from our goal. Another crew is working the Smith River–Coal River strip (one over which we are traveling now) while the Captain and his crew work up from Lower Post. Thus two weeks more of "road" locating lie ahead.*

*It has been raining steadily for two days now, and we're all anxious to get it over with. The walk today was a hard one, taking all day. Most of it was over the rocky bank of the Liard. Swarms of cranes filled the skies, preparing for their flight down south. And so will we, soon...*

*August 27, 1942          Thursday          On the Liard*

*I've been taking some beatings lately; am run down to such an extent I don't know if I'll make it to the end. My eyes especially. Just now the left one is almost closed giving me pain. I scratched it in the dense spruce thicket yesterday.*

*Our man Jennerjahn returned from a two day hunting trip with the large heart of a moose. The carcass is too far away to be worth while sending for. We're in the Liard rapids where the water churns and roars as it flows over the rocks. A very rugged and picturesque country indeed.*

*August 28, 1942*        *Friday*        *On the Liard*

Just now I'm smoking my last cigarette. The supply is gone and we won't
have any more until we've finished this job.

Little chow left for the remaining fifteen days. Maybe we'll be lucky to get
a moose. There should be enough fish, tho.

The nights are long now, and first rays of Aurora Borealis have shown them
selves. There was a complete eclipse of the moon the other night; it was a full
moon, and there was something weird in the sight.

*August 29, 1942*        *Saturday*        *On the Liard*

The river is shallow now, and rather wide. The Army sea plane is circling
overhead; they're keeping track of our camp so that they can bring us chow...

*September 4, 1942*        *Friday*        *On the Liard*

Our remaining aerial photos show approximately 8 more miles of road.
Today both parties hit a lucky streak, making two miles apiece; that's almost 3 miles
more than our average for the last week.

Last Sunday the plane landed on the river with our chow and a month's
mail. John sent a camera and I've taken a number of pictures. The country, however, is not spectacular any more. On the way back I'll try to recapture some of the
splendor that I saw there.

*September 10, 1942*        *Thursday*

The line tied in today!

After a two-day burst of energy, we finally tied into Captain Eschbach's
line. Lots of backslapping and handshaking; movie cameras (officers' and Spain's)
clicked, and shutters snapped. I took some myself. Tomorrow the combined parties
start the journey "home" to our base camp. It shouldn't take over a week. The
chow's almost gone again, about time we got back to regular meals for a change.

Celebrating the "tie in" near Contact Creek.

95

Adolph Adrian catches up on the wash.

Shave and a haircut... two bits.

*September 17, 1942      Thursday      Base Camp - Liard River*

*Three meals a day again. Not much to do but sleep and eat, wash laundry and do some reading.*

*We caused quite a riot when we hit the clearing. Everyone was out with cameras taking pictures of our wild hair and unshaven faces. And in the base camp, the same happened, with handshaking of buddies that we hadn't seen for four months.*

*Now that we've all had our hair-cuts, we feel half civilized again, wondering what will happen to us next. Next week we begin "school" to refresh our minds on the rudiments of surveying. Then we may go to the field or else return to Nelson or Fort St. John. At any rate, our departure from Canada won't come about until the road— or the clearing —is completed, and a third-order survey line run over it to the Lower Post.*

*September 21, 1942      Monday      Camp Liard*

*Fall is here in all its glory; in the brilliant sun of an Indian summer day, the falling leaves are like a shower of gold. It's as though Nature treated herself to one last fling before taking on the somber garb of winter.*

*The tent is full of poker players and cigarette smoke. The gas lamp sways—and now and then someone stands in front of it, cutting me off from the light. No more letters to write; they were all written days ago.*

*"A pair of deuces, three of a kind, a flush!"—and so on into the night.*

96

## CRAMBLITT, THE BEAR AND OTHER STORIES

After my sojourn to Muncho Lake, we passed a lot of sliding rock along the Racing River. It was there that P. Peterson shot at a brown bear and missed. Word of this encounter got back to Cramblitt, and he then decided to leave the reconnaissance party, and go back to construction. He was deathly afraid of bears.

A week or so later, I broke out with yellow jaundice, and had to go back to see a doctor. After two days and two horses, I had come to the head of the road, and was feeling good again. Captain Stewart had me wait for supplies and mail.

As I was lying around, I saw Cramblitt go into the latrine. It was a pit, measuring five by eight feet, with eight holes, four to a side. Cramblitt must have gone on the far side, because just then a bear entered the latrine door. I called Captain Stewart's attention to what was about to happen.

Suddenly, there was a blood-curdling scream, and Cramblitt streaked out the door, his trousers around his ankles. How he got past the

Bob Cramblitt

bear I will never know. He hobbled right over to Stewart, and told him he was going back to the reconnaissance with me.

At the camp there happened to be a 35th Engineers PX truck, so I bought some candy bars for my crew and then noticed a roll of Copenhagen snuff. On a hunch, I picked it up, as I knew Arky Tolleson could use it.

When we got back to camp everyone wanted their mail, so I got it off the pack horse. The mail included another package for Tolleson. On opening it, he reacted as before, cussing and throwing soap up into the trees. I asked him what was wrong. Spiegel said that Arky was having a nicotine fit.

I then told Arky that I had a tin of snuff for him in my bedroll. Tolleson unloaded the whole pack string before he got to my bedroll.

Then it dawned on him that he should pay for it. I told him the snuff would cost $20, just to see if he would pay it. He didn't have the money at the time, but he tried to give me $20 about a month later. I then told him the snuff cost 60 cents, which he paid. I then asked him how much he would have paid for it, and he said $100.

We paralleled the Liard River all the way to the Hudson Bay Lower Post. There the lieutenant lost the toes of his shoes in a camp fire. How he managed to do it without burning his toes I'll never know. We hailed McPhie, and he landed his plane on the river. We ordered the lieutenant some shoes, and a couple days later McPhie dropped them in the trees. We never did find them.

McPhie's Norseman on Mucho Lake

Upon arriving at Muncho Lake, a bush pilot by the name of McPhie brought his Norseman float plane down on the lake. He told us he was to fly us to Watson Lake for the best dinner that money could buy at Army expense. It took us a little over an hour to fly from Muncho Lake to Watson Lake. It had taken us over a month of walking to locate the road over the same distance.

On the way back to Muncho Lake, McPhie took us east of the Liard River crossing to the Grand Canyon of the Liard, where the river goes through a canyon only 24 feet wide. At the road crossing, the river is nearly 2,000 feet wide.

Pete Peterson told us that a man named Tom Smith and his daughter had once tried to raft the narrows of the Liard with their winter catch of furs. The raft overturned, Smith was drowned and the furs lost. The daughter survived, having been washed up on a sandbar. Later on, she worked at Fort Nelson. She told Peterson that their trapping cabin was in the valley, where it never froze. It was the first we had heard of one of the famous tropical valleys of the arctic.

When we reached the Liard River, we had to make the horses swim, and built a raft to cross. A mile or so from the crossing, we came upon a trapping cabin used by Pete Peterson, John Olds and Tom Smith. On the table was a note from John Olds. It said "The plice (sic) have finally come for me, I do not know when I will be back, there is moose cached up my trail 20 minutes."

The police were after him because he had been trapping on land reserved for the Indians. However, they wouldn't go there, because it had been a very large forest with young trees eight to ten feet tall, making it a regular jungle. Large dead trees also were all over the place, making it even worse. One stretch of it took us eight hours to traverse. After a caterpillar tractor went through behind us, we walked back in about half an hour.

Chris Gras

## TRAIL OF THE YUKON

One day the lieutenant, Petersen and Louie Police moved our camp up the river while we blazed the location for the road. They moved the camp a little farther than we had blazed the trail, so we walked over to the river and saw the horse tracks and followed them to camp.

When we got there, the lieutenant wanted to know how we had found the camp. I told him on account of the horses. He asked which horse told us, and we went along with his joke and told him the white one. He then said, "Well, you were lucky to find the camp, because you can't believe a thing the white horse says."

Near the Smith River, on the Liard, we came upon a large sand bar. Petersen said it was called The Million Dollar Bar because there was supposed to be a lot of gold buried there. At Smith River there had once been a trading post at one time. We found a broken scale, but it was the only evidence of the 1898 store on the "Inland Klondike Trail."

Chris Gras

## THE LAST BLAZE

Late in the evening of September 7, as rain drenched our camp on the cliffs above the Liard, at Forty Mile Canyon, Lt. Stewart walked into Capt. Eschbach's camp, thus joining the two parties. The next day the two homesick Indians deserted with their pack strings and returned to Lower Post.

At last, after a day's hard push, the two lines were formally joined in a field of scrubby spruce. It was a brilliant sunny day, and standing around the last tree to be blazed were Capt. Eschbach, Capt. L. M. Stewart, Lt. L. Lancaster and Capt. Bolen of the 35th Engineer's Regiment, together with nearly all of the men of the recon parties.

The last tree was blazed by Sgts. Gras and Halfacre, with several

Lancaster and Stewart shake hands as the two parties "tie in."

cameras recording the event. Then with the suddenness of a tropical sunset, the job was ended, the long uphill fight was won, and there remained nothing more but some revision work and the two-day hike back to the head of the advancing road.

Chris Gras

## SNAPSHOTS FROM A SOLDIER'S SCRAPBOOK

"Load 'em up move 'em out."

Another pack-train sets out.

Corduroy ...one
tough way to build a road.

Progress underway...

"We'll worry about the
bridges later."

Rebuilding the Kledo bridge
after floods.

Crossing Steamboat creek.

Pontoon bridge over Toad River.

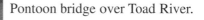

Moving men & equipment -
Liard River.

Walter Church (on left)
and buddies.

**PHOTOS FROM WALTER CHURCH COLLECTION
CO "A" - 35TH COMBAT ENGINEERS**

## RECOLLECTIONS

I may know how geese decide when it is time to start south from the arctic. In early September I was camping on the Coal River when I first saw the northern lights put on their brilliant display. Up until this time I had seen few geese, but that night they began coming into the mouth of the river from the north, and soon the sand bars were covered solid with them. They were very noisy. In two days they had gone south, and it started to freeze. I believe the northern lights may be a signal to them that it is time to move south.

There were many birds; ptarmigan and grouse were plentiful and the raven was ever-present. Bees were a source of honey for bears, and the Indians and we often saw evidence of their hives in hollow trees along the trail. The blue jays were notorious camp robbers. The Indians said of them, "Him Hudson's Bay jay." "Why?" we asked. "Just like Hudson's Bay—him steal from everybody!"

An important lesson we learned: never lasso a bear! One bear kept coming around our kitchen truck at the base camp, so one of the soldiers thought it would be fun to try to rope him. He improvised a lariat, tied the end to the truck and, throwing a loop at the bear, caught him. That was one mad bear! He was rampaging around so much we could not get close enough to the truck to cut the rope. No kitchen truck—no food, so reluctantly I had to order him shot.

The construction of the road disoriented geese and sand cranes, and as the landscape changed, they would fly up and down in erratic patterns, their landmarks altered, puzzled by the big gash through their woods.

Black flies, horseflies and little gnats called "no-see-ums" were a continual source of torment. Big mosquitoes were legendary and mosquito bars were an absolute necessity, day and night. The story was that when two mosquitoes landed on a soldier, one said to the other, "Hey, let's take him back to the swamp!" "No," said the other, "if we do that the big guys will take him away from us."

Under such primitive conditions food becomes very important to a man's morale. As a rule, we did not shoot game because that would delay our work. However, we did set fish lines at night, hoping to catch fresh fish. A typical break-fast at our base camp would be oatmeal mush with dried milk, scrambled powdered eggs with ham, fresh fish (possibly) and soda biscuits. Noon meals consisted of tea, biscuits and ham, and at night we would have dehydrated potatoes, powdered eggs, ham and coffee.

Alfred M. Eschbach
Commanding Officer
Co. "A" 648th Engineers

# CHAPTER X

# MUNCHO LAKE TO CONTACT CREEK
# HARRY'S LETTERS HOME

*August 9, 1942*                                    *Camp on Muncho Lake, B.C.,*
                                                    *Canada*

*While on our two-day journey, the plane in which our little party arrived, was by no means idle. The pilot and the mechanic picked up Sgt. Gras and our lieutenant at the further end of the lake and flew them up over the proposed route to a settlement at Lower Post at the end of our job. There Sgt. Gras bought a few things at a Hudson Bay store. He brought me back two bottles of citronella which helps check the gnats and $5 worth of 5 cent candy bars. Up here, where everything has to be flown in, candy bars sell three for a quarter. I certainly was happy to get them. I eat about three bars a day. What luxury! I also have a pair of moose hide moccasins. I got them from a trapper who is guiding our recon party. They came from a Hudson Bay Store and cost me $1.50. They sure are comfortable to wear around the camp evenings.*

*The biggest thrill came the evening we returned from our pack trip to the Lake. I had just finished the supper dishes, when the major asked Tolleson and me if we would like to fly down to the other end of the Lake where Sgt. Gras and the lieutenant were that evening. I could hardly believe my ears! We were two proud boys as we climbed into the cabin of the neat little plane with the pilot. I could write on and on describing taxiing out over the deep blue water and the thrilling take off. What an incredible and spectacular terrain from the air! We circled once over Gras' camp, landed perfectly, and taxied to shore. The Sgt. and the lieutenant were surprised to see us! They both had their movie cameras in operation, and took pictures of our landing, a group picture of us standing on the pontoons, and the take-off again.*

*We flew back to our camp that night, and the next morning my partner and I had a still more pleasant surprise. The major asked us to fly with him down to the Liard River, the largest river our route crosses. What a*

Float plane on the Liard River.

*thrilling flight thru a beautiful wilderness valley paralleled by a rugged mountain range on either side. We landed on the river and docked on a rockbound shore at a lonely trapper's cabin. What a peaceful spot far away from the cares and heartaches of our war-torn world!*

*We cached a lot of supplies in the cabin which our party will pick up when we advance that far. After storing the chow in the cabin, we boarded the plane and flew down the river to a possible landing site. Tolleson and I took depth measurements from the left pontoon. The pilot taxied diagonally across the river and we took readings as quickly as possible calling the depths to the major who recorded them. We repeated this process three times to get a "mean." This done, we took off again and finally landed back on the jeweled lake at our camp. We had lunch and the major and his party left us. Before he left he thanked us for our kindness and bade us "good luck." He and his party sure were good to Tolleson and me. I will never forget them.*

*The next day we rejoined our party. Our comrades were thrilled to hear we had a couple of flights in the major's seaplane. We were two lucky boys to have had such a wonderful experience! I forgot to mention when the plane first arrived they brought along two heads of fresh lettuce. What a treat! We put them into a cold, bubbling spring along the shoreline of the lake for a few minutes, and the lettuce became nice and crisp. I don't believe anything tasted more delicious. I can't say much about the progress of our job, but morale is high and things are happening fast!*

*August 14, 1942*                          *Camp on Trout River, B.C., Canada*

*The weather is ideal up here now. There is a hint of fall in the air, and the gnats haven't been so bad the last few days. There are wolves in this valley we are working thru. Our rations are becoming monotonous.*

*August 18, 1942        Tuesday        Camp on Liard River, B.C., Canada*

There is a slight touch of fall in this country now. Some of the leaves are already beginning to turn yellow and fall from the trees and brush in the lowlands along the river beds. The days are pleasantly warm, and the nights are refreshingly cool. The final push for our recon party is on.

Somehow, ever since we started out, something unusual and eventful happens on every Sabbath. Last Sunday was no exception, because we hit the Liard River, the largest in this area. This big, muddy river with its treacherous currents boiling and eddying to the top as it moves along, reminds me a great deal of the Mississippi.

The proposed location is on the opposite side, and as our little outfit was the first to reach the river, it was necessary for us to cut timber and construct two large rafts. We chopped out a number of rough paddles and were ready to begin the tedious task of ferrying all our supplies, equipment, and personnel across. It took three men paddling to handle each raft. It was a steady pull and due to current we always landed about a fifth of a mile downstream on the opposite side. A detail of five men would unload the raft and with a long lead line pull the raft upstream for the return trip back to the other shore for another load of freight. The towing detail made quite a sight as they pulled up the rocky shore to a chorus of "Volga Boatman"! I got a big kick out of that bit of comedy.

It took the best part of the day to get all our supplies and the men ferried across the river. We were glad to get everything safely over including all the panniers, saddles, cinches, etc., but the biggest thrill was when the horses were stripped, herded into the water and driven across the river. We whooped and hollered and threw stones which splashed just behind them. They plunged in readily and began to swim, but when the current hit them, the lead horse became frightened and turned back. Bellowing like Indians on the war path, we ran down the shore trying to head the snorting, tuckered horses back into the main channel. Our efforts were in vain, and they came back to shore. I felt sorry for them.

One of the trappers who is wrangling for our outfit has two dogs along with him. "Sandy," the lead dog in Cliff's dog team, is a pretty smart canine and a friend to all the men in our outfit. After the horses rested, we again started them across. This time Sandy plunged in after them. Whenever the horses attempted to turn back, he was right behind them, barking and yipping for all he was worth. His efforts did the trick; the horses swam all the way. The last hundred feet Sandy rode on the back of one of the big mares as she swam. That dog was proud of himself and rightly so. The filly was among the horses, and acted like a veteran for she is becoming a grown young lady now. We finally got everyone and everything safely over the big river. We had a hard time keeping Sandy from swimming back and forth across the river every time the ferry made a trip. As it was, he made about four crossings. He sure was one tired dog at night.

*Somehow on this job, I always seem to be in on the more exciting happenings. Once across the river, the recon and survey parties took off the following morning, but the lieutenant and I were left behind. I had to select a couple of day's chow and necessary pots and pans. We two camped here beside the river awaiting the appearance of the lead "cats" on the opposite shore. In the meantime, we are taking it easy, just waiting for a light pontoon boat powered by a 22 horsepower Johnson outboard motor. We will load our camp equipment into the boat and take off up river. About ten miles up we will locate the survey party's camp and dock there. The following morning we plan to start out again in our boat with a line crew. We are supposed to proceed up the Liard about 30 miles and then start running a line. With this system our undertaking will be completed sooner, because a number of crews will be working from different points and tie into each other. I am pleased to be going ahead with the advance crew again. What experiences I am having!*

*The latest rumor afloat regards our next assignment. The story is based on a few newspaper articles regarding another road job. If there is any truth to this, it would suit me fine, because it would be non-combative work, still in this hemisphere, only in the opposite direction.*

*August 26, 1942*                 *Camp on the Liard River, B.C., Canada*

*Fall is in the air. The leaves are changing color and the nights are snappy. Last night we had an almost total eclipse of the full moon. Already the northern lights are putting on displays each night. I had another ride in the pontoon plane. A number of ten pound pike were caught recently. They sure are tasty eating. This job is really blitzing now. We are definitely out of the Rockies.*

*September 1, 1942*    *Monday*        *Camp on the Liard River, B.C., Canada*

*I wrote that a lieutenant and I were waiting for a pontoon boat to go up the river. We didn't get the expected boat, because they were all needed to ferry supplies. Instead, we had another ride in the pontoon plane. That suited me to a "T." We landed on the river when spotting the survey party's pack outfit and picked up some aerial photographs needed. We took off again and landed where our party awaited us.*

*It was quite an experience waiting for the head of the clearing to be pushed thru down to the river. Our line had been blazed thru the wilderness to that point for a number of days. The lieutenant and I waited and heard and saw nothing until the second day. First we heard the distant drone of the big D8 "cats." As they progressed around the mountain, the roar became louder and louder until finally the lead "cat" crashed thru the brush pushing giant trees over like match sticks, and clattered down to the river's edge. Believe it or not, in less than an hour, loaded trucks were rolling down onto the gravel river bed. Loads of lumber were soon stacked up, pontoon trailers swung into place, powerful motors were unloaded and in jig time assault boats were puttering across the river and a ferry site selected.*

*In a short time, loads of lumber (milled right in these woods by Army boys) and tools were coming across the river in pontoon boats with big, powerful motors chugging behind, whipping the current into foam. Portable arc lights were set up on both shores and work continued all thru the night. By breakfast time the following morning, the approaches were finished, a big six ferry boat had been completed, and the job of ferrying the "cats," trucks, graders, etc. was about to begin. The big pontoon ferry anchored at the camp with six big motors behind was an impressive sight. All in all, I was impressed by the efficiency of Uncle Sam's army engineers.*

Ferrying a D-8 "cat" acoss the Liard River.
(Photo courtesy - Walter Church - 35th Eng.)

*The first day of September gave us a white, frosty morning. The morning air was invigorating, the afternoon warm and balmy, and after a great day this is truly a beautiful, peaceful evening as I sit here by the river's edge. The last few nights after dark, wolves howled again and last night we heard a moose call. Their mating season starts shortly.*

*We have been enjoying a beautiful moon. One night we had an eclipse of the moon. It was quite a spectacle. I had never really seen one before. On some nights we see displays of northern lights and our days are getting shorter. It's quite dark by nine o'clock each evening.*

The combined pack outfits of the recon and survey parties.

*September 15, 1942    Tuesday         Base Survey Camp*

*After battling the remote wilderness day in and day out since the middle of last April, a few days ago we tied in the centerline on our sector, completing the mission. On the day we finished the line it was exactly six months to the day our troop train crossed the border and entered Canada. Amidst the cheers of the two parties, which had been working the centerline toward each other, the last tree was blazed and the gap was linked. I was thrilled! To me the event was comparable to the driving of the Golden Spike when the Union Pacific Railroad was completed across our glorious West in 1869.*

*Quite a few of the fellows had their cameras with them when we tied in the line, and took some good snaps. The Reconnaissance and the Survey Parties were combined, and the following day, started our long trek back to the head of the road. The combined pack outfit made a string of horses about fifty in number! All the fellows were in jubilant spirits as we hiked back even though averaging fifteen miles a day. On the morning of the third day, while packing, blasting was heard. We knew we were getting close to the lead "cats." About noon, rounding a point on the river, we could see the dust and hear the roar of the D-8's clawing their way thru the wilderness toward us.*

*As I walked down the road I was thrilled and more than a little proud to have had a part in this great job. What a few days before had been only a series of well-chosen blazes on trees, is not a highway, still rough, but passable. Such an incredible transformation had taken place I found it very difficult to locate and identify topography I had noticed when the road was still "bush."*

*We were a sight, lightly stepping along the road. With our long hair, whiskers, torn clothes and worn shoes we looked as if we were heading for a hobo's convention. When the horses hit the clearing they broke into a run instead of plodding along as they usually did on the trail. It was a great day* for both man and beast. The trapper's two dogs who had been with us all summer were so excited they ran up and down the road beside the horses yipping and barking happily.

All the construction boys we met were eager to hear about our experiences up ahead, and of course, we were anxious to hear all the dope they had. Many gave us candy bars, which were a welcome treat. We rode back to the survey camp in a GI truck. The ride was plenty rough, but another comparatively new experience. What hearty welcomes were received from our old buddies at this camp! All kinds of pictures were taken, both snaps and movies. Compared to the monotonous rations in the field what wonderful chow was served. We had soup, fresh baked bread, fresh vegetables and fresh meat. Food never tasted so good! Even though I didn't lose much weight during the summer, I know I'm going to gain weight on these rations.

Today they are letting us take it easy and rest up. I got a good haircut from the company barber, shaved, cleaned up and straightened out my belongings, so I feel like a normal human once more, and must admit it feels great!

Production on the home front must be in high gear now, judging from the swarms of bombers and pursuit planes flying over here, undoubtedly laden with presents for our Asian friends. From what little war news I can gather, my guess is all hell will break loose before long.

I don't know as yet what we are going to do now. We might either revise some of the line, help this outfit survey the finished road, or go back and start crating our equipment. The weather is starting to get pretty snappy. We have frost almost every night. Back at one lake at a high elevation there is a foot of snow reported. During the day and night flocks of ducks, geese, and swans noisily pass overhead honking and winging their way southward ahead of the cold weather. The stage is being set for "Old Man Winter."

Col Russell Lyons of the 340th Engineers and Col. James McCarty (right) of the
35th Combat Engineers - meet at Contact Creek.

*September 16, 1942    Wednesday    Base Survey Camp*

*A few days ago we tied in the line, thereby completing our mission.
It certainly was a thrill when the final blaze was whacked, thus completing
the long, weary, but most interesting months in this remote wilderness so
far from civilization.*

*When finally reaching the head of the clearing, I found it almost
impossible to comprehend the transformation that had taken place. This
highway will certainly be something for our nations to be proud of when it is
finished. The army boys in overalls are really making a name for themselves. The politicians in Washington who opposed this job will be singing a
different tune before long. As my lieutenant said, "This highway will cost less
than a battleship, cannot be sunk, and will be a thing of joy and beauty
forever."*

*[Editors note—The above photograph and passage from "Harry's letter home"
have been engraved in granite on the Alaska Highway Veterans and Builders
Monument unveiled and dedicated June 26th, 2004 at the Fort Nelson Heritage
Museum.  Helen Navratil and children and Sgt. Chris Gras' daughters and their
family were in attendance as special guests. ]*

*September 17, 1942*

We fellows in the location parties that returned from the "bush" are still "taking it easy" here at this camp. Today the Captain told us that Monday morning we are going to organize and attend school classes at our camp here reviewing old and taking up new work on the principals of highway surveying. There I imagine we will become a second survey crew and two shifts we be run. This news suits me to a tee! Just think how fortunate I am to be able to attend school classes and work up here in this peaceful country, when the majority of our other soldiers are engaged in bitter conflicts now raging in dozens of places all over the globe. I am indeed fortunate! Even though advancement comes very slowly in a Topo unit, because it is such a high technical organization, being a member of one certainly has its merits.

In spite of the misimpressions I must have unknowingly imprinted on your minds, this job isn't complicated yet by a long shot, and we expect to be up here for quite a spell yet. As a matter of fact yesterday a truck was sent way back to our supply base at Fort Nelson to fetch out our arctic winter clothing. That speaks almost for itself. If only I could speak more freely and state more facts and figures about the job, I could more easily calm what fears you may be harbouring.

*September 23, 1942*               *Survey Camp on the "Alcan Highway"*
                                   *B.C., Canada*

Well, since we returned from the "bush" we have rested up, and we are now doing our bit again. A second shift survey crew has been organized. I am now working in the computer's section for our "Operations Dept.." Here the figures are tabulated in the recording books of the transit, level and taping parties computes. This information is then used as "control" for the map making.

Computing requires a pretty fair knowledge of advanced mathematics. Believe me I am getting a fair bit of dust knocked off my brain. The experience is good for me, because I am not only "brushing up," but I am learning a lot of new things too. The work I am doing at present is giving me a very clear insight as to what this topographic surveying is all about, and just how many of these almost incredible results are delivered.

Night crews "shoot" Polaris (North Star) and therefore an exact location is determined. The computation necessary to locate the position sure is a "honey." A fellow has to be an Einstein to dope it out., I hope to be able to master that computation before this is all over.

The weather up here is ideal again, in spite of the fact that we had a cold rainy spell last week during which a few snow flurries fell. The days are clear and cool and the moonlit nights are simply beautiful. Then along about bed-time each night "old mother nature" starts to put on her display of

*Northern Lights, in ever changing and pulsating bands of colour in white, yellow, green and blue. For this time of the year up here, the weather sure is swell.*

*Except for a few P.X. items, there is no way to spend money up here at all. All the fellows are toting around a wad of "cabbage" big enough to choke a horse. Each night many of the tents become miniature "Monte Carlos." The favourite games are Black Jack, Stud poker and Red Dog.*

*September 23, 1942*                    *Survey Camp on the "Alcan Highway"*
                                         *B.C., Canada*

*We are now in the midst of a shake-up of the officer personnel in our company. Our captain bade us farewell today. It is rumoured that he might be promoted to major soon. We are also going to get a lieutenant in our outfit soon. I hope that our new officers will be decent fellows and agreeable to work under.*

*Here's a tale I should have related in a past letter about 6 weeks ago when it happened, but some how it slipped my mind. One of the construction boys on the road was walking down the road after the caterpillar had gone thru. A tall spruce was leaning at an angle over the road and as this fellow walked under it, it fell and a large limb struck him on the head knocking him unconscious. He had a fractured skull. He was left on the spot and a small wall tent erected over his limp form right in the center of the road. Traffic and construction went on outside his tent. By the time that the doctor arrived a blood clot formed on his brain. Even though the doctor had no tools for such a major operation, there was only one chance—he had to operate. This may sound like a tall one, but I swear and can prove that it's the gospel truth, Mom and Dad. After he had sterilized them in boiling water, with the aid of two construction officers, he performed the operation with a bit of brace, a hack-saw blade, a chisel and a hammer. These tools were all from a carpenter's chest. After a few days the boy regained consciousness and he rallied. He was then flown by plane to a hospital back in the states. He was doing fine and then a few days ago we received the terrible news that he took a turn for the worst and died. That was a blow to all of us because we were all hoping and praying that he would pull thru.*

*****

[Editors note—The following passage, corroberating the emergency roadside brain surgery is taken from Chester L Russell's "Tales of a Catskinner - A Personal Account of Building the Alaska Highway, The Winter Trail, and Canol Pipeline Road in 1942 -43" pages 40-42. Used with permission of the author.]

## MOORE'S BRAIN OPERATION

One day, Sgt. Bailey and his trailblazing crew of Moore, James Grice, and Lawrence Loftin were walking back to camp, following behind the Cats at what I thought was a safe distance. We were bulldozing trees and clearing the right of way, as usual, when suddenly a tree limb came back over the top of the tractor, hitting Moore on the head and knocking him unconscious. We worked for quite some time trying to bring him to, but we were not successful. Using a command car equipped with a Morse code unit for sending and receiving messages, our wireless operator sent a message to Dr. Stotts back at main camp, reporting the accident and our need of medical assistance. It took the doctor quite some time to get to us. Road conditions were poor and his jeep got stuck in the mud after only two miles of driving. He had to walk the rest of the way, about three to four miles, before he reached us at the scene of Moore's accident.

When he got there, he kneeled down beside Moore, and the first thing he did was check Moore's eyes. Then Dr. Stotts looked up at us and said, "Fellows, Moore has a clot on the brain." As he held Moore's left eyelid open, he showed us that this eye was clear, meaning no injury. Then he opened the right eyelid, and to me it looked as if there was no life in it. Dr. Stotts explained to all of us where he thought the blood clot was most likely to be located, which was on the other side of Moore's head, behind the left ear.

"There are several blood vessels that cross over each other like railroad tracks," I recall was the way that the doctor described it. These has been injured and were releasing blood into Moore's skull. His condition required immediate action, and the doctor advised us that Moore would never survive an evacuation to better medical facilities. "There is no way that we can get him out of here in time to save him, but if you fellows are willing to help me, we can operate here," he said. We told him that we would do whatever he asked.

Naturally he didn't have with him the proper surgical equipment or facilities to deal with such a medical emergency. Circumstances in the wilderness forced the doctor to make-do with the simple handtools that we could provide a wood brace with 3/8-inch bit, a piece of hacksaw blade, a pair of pliers and a syringe of his own. I don't remember if Dr. Stotts used his own surgical knives or if he used one of our razor blades, but I think he used the latter. I do know that he did a neat job of laying the skin back before drilling three holes in a triangular pattern into Moore's skull. Grasping the piece of hacksaw blade with the pliers, he sawed out the bone between the holes. It wasn't long after that when Dr. Stotts announced that the pressure had been released, and a sigh of relief could be heard from each of us. Then we got busy carefully clearing away all the fallen limbs and brush in the general area where Moore lay, lifting him onto a cot, and then erecting a tent over him to protect him from the elements.

The doctor stayed at our Cat Camp to attend to Moore while he was recovering, during which time we returned to our own work of building the road. Then, on the fourth day, the doctor sent word to us that fluid was filling Moore's lungs, and that now this threatened to kill him. Officer Ammon asked the Doctor why we couldn't rig up an air compressor to suck the fluid from Moore's lungs. Doc answered Ammon that it should be done if it was possible to build it. Well, they made the rig, and the doctor removed that dangerous fluid. Several more days went by before I got a chance to visit with Moore. When I saw him, he was sitting up, feeling pretty good, and we even talked for a while.

After word got back to main camp about that risky operation in the field, some staff officers arrived by plane and insisted on flying Moore to Seattle for more orthodox medical treatment. He died en route, three hours before getting there. Dr. Stotts told us that if they would have let Moore stay at the Cat camp and allowed him to fully recover, he would be alive today. In his opinion, the effects of stress and pressure changes caused by flying Moore out in an unpressurized airplane were what killed Moore.

*****

September 25, 1942

Survey Camp on the Alcan Highway
B.C., Canada

We were busy computing in the Operations tent this afternoon, when a notice was put up on the bulletin board. Twelve fellows are listed to start out back down the highway about 50 miles in the morning to lay out an emergency landing field for airplanes. I am one of the party. The lieutenant that I worked under on reconnaissance this summer is in charge of the party. I am to work the plane-table plotting elevations with contours. I did a little of this work in training back at camp Claiborne, last Winter. This little job promises to be an interesting one. I certainly am fortunate that I am getting jobs in various phases of survey work and therefore it never gets monotonous. I can't reveal any details about the highway or this layout job we're going on, but by putting 2 and 2 together and from what you read in your daily papers, you can formulate a pretty clear picture in your mind of developments here.

The pyramid tent "Alcan Hilton."

*We 12 fellows are taking 2 large pyramid tents with us and all of our personal equipment. We will chow with a construction outfit down there that has a reputation for dishing out good grub. They have good mailing facilities there too, so I will drop you a few lines from our camp and let you know how I am getting along.*

*Wednesday Evening*
*September 30, 1942*                    *Survey Camp on "Alcan Highway"*
                                        *B.C., Canada*

*Tonight I am at leisure, so I will relax and spell off a few lines and thereby chat with you. I am sitting on the edge of my bunk here in our pyramidal tent writing by the light of a Coleman gasoline lantern hanging on the centre pole. A good fire is glowing in our little Sibley tent stove, so all is quite snug and comfy. My four tent mates complete the family circle as they are passing this evening shaving up, reading writing letters, spinning yarns, or just resting.*

*We have had no snow to amount to anything as yet, but we are ready for it, because a few days ago our arctic clothes were sent up to us from summer storage.*

*I still can't say much about our job up here, but a few days ago the "cats" broke thru on our sector. I am told that they even had a four-piece band playing out there on the occasion. The event was the realization of a dream that every man in these parts has been harbouring since the first tree*

115

*was uprooted last spring. The magnitude of this undertaking is almost incredible. My life's biggest ambition now is to someday when this terrible war has ended, to take an automobile trip on this road all the way through to Alaska. What a wonderful trip that would be, and there's not a reason in the world why it can't become a realization.*

*Even though we are far from civilization up here, we have our good times. Some evenings about 25 fellows all pile into one tent and there by candlelight we have a sing fest. Some of the fellows solo and then the whole shebang joins in. The boys like the little ditty about the "Harlem Goat." No jam session is complete without singing that one. Some of these guys are born comedians, and they sure can pull sidesplitting gags.*

*October 2, 1942*                              *Survey Camp on "Alcan Highway" B.C., Canada*

*What a wonderful trip we had down here. We rode down in a carry-all (station-wagon). I could not believe my eyes when I saw the wonderful shape that the road is in. It's really marvellous. What a scenic drive this highway affords as it winds along the tumbling streams and thru the silent mountains. Just to give you an idea in what good shape this road is, when we came down here, in stretches we cruised along at 50 m.p.h. with ease. After not riding in an automobile since last Spring that trip was quite a thrill. Now I know that one of my life's biggest ambitions is someday for all of us to take a trip up thru this country together.*

*Our work here is progressing quite well. We have finished one survey and we are going to start working on another landing field tomorrow. I am doing the drafting; plotting the controls & profiles and making the necessary sketches. I find this quite interesting work, which also is a good experience for me.*

*I wish that you could see the bridge that these boys built across the Liard River near here. It is constructed wholly of timber cut of these mountain sides and lumber buzzed up in the G.I. saw mills set up right in the "bush," and operated by soldiers. The bridge foundations are all pile driven. Again I wish that I could give you some impressing facts and figures, but I cannot. This river is comparable to the Mississippi in many respects so you can imagine what an under- taking it was to bridge it. I get a thrill every time I cross it, because it certainly is a masterpiece of pioneer engineering. It's difficult for me to realize that I rafted across*

G.I. built bridge across the Liard. *this river.*

*This I found almost impossible to believe myself, but a few days ago I saw a number of new trucks loaded with freight rolling thru, bearing signs in front reading. "Fairbanks Freight!" That speaks for itself!*

October 13, 1942                    Survey Camp on "Alcan Highway" B.C., Canada

Liard Hotsprings - "C'mon in, the water's fine."

*Although there is still no snow in the lowlands, the surrounding majestic mountains are now garbed in a coat of crystal white. How beautiful, how majestic they stand keeping their silent watch over this vast country. At breakfast the rising sun is just chinning itself over the range and giving birth to a new day. The sunrises and sunsets are a vivid splash of colour. The nights are clear, cold and still and the sky is a glittering mass of frosty twinkling "jewels."*

*No mom, we don't have any shower facilities up here at these camps. We take a bath in a bucket of water once in a while. However there is a hot spring not far from this camp similar to those we saw in Yellowstone. The water temperature is about 100 degrees Fahrenheit. Tomorrow a group of us are going up there for a real bath.*

*There is a chaplain at this camp. Last Sunday morning I attended my first church service since last Easter. We fellows sat on canvas tarps spread on the company strut. I enjoyed the service immensely. The band had a short concert preceding the service and they played hymns during the program. I can't describe how fully I enjoyed it all.*

October 23, 1942                    Camp on "Alcan Highway" B.C., Canada

*Today I had a real treat that I kept wishing you could have shared with me. A few miles from this camp on the mountainside about 1/3 of a mile from the highway is a hot spring. What a strange phenomenon of nature! I walked there and back on the road. By golly, there is so much traffic on the*

road already, that it's almost as bad as when we used to take a hike along the highways back home; every few minutes some vehicle stops and you are offered a ride. By working evenings I got caught up on my work, so this afternoon I went up to the springs for a bath. As it was early I was the only one there, so I had the whole pool to myself. Picture the hot springs we once saw in Yellowstone. This spring is almost identical in nature, except that it doesn't emit the nauseating rotten-egg fumes as those springs did. This one has but a very slight sulphur smell. It is a large pool about 45 feet in diameter. In the chill of the clear October air the whole   surface of the water pleasantly steams. The center of the pool is constantly bubbling replenishing Nature's bathtub with clean warm water from the  bowels of the earth. The water is grey blue in colour and at an ideal temperature of about 100 degrees fahrenheit. Look the mythed wood nymph, I got into my birthday suit on the timbered edge of the pool and strode in! It's soothing warmth was great! What a swell bath I took! The water was very hard though, and it was difficult to get a lather from the soap.

I basked in the hot springs all of an hour before I reluctantly came out. And say, that pool is deep too. I swam to the center and dove down about 15 feet and still no bottom. The water got hotter down deeper too. I came up kind of quick because I was afraid that old Satan himself might grab me by the big toe and take me down to the fire boilers!

Under the light of a full moon and a star-studded sky, the last few nites in particular have been simply beautiful.  A couple of times each evening I go out of my tent and stand alone in the invigorating nite air and admire, yes almost worship the view of the snowy mountain ranges in the distance, a whitest of white against the back-drop of nite as they are bathed in moonlight.  It's not only the incredible view, but many other physical stimulus' that make it all so wonderful—the chill of the quiet nite, the smell of the frosted pine and tamarack, and except for the eiry hush of the nearby river as it moves its way to the Arctic, ice-bound wastes, the silence, the peace, the solitude.

Our winter camp along the Alcan.

*In my letters you probably get tired of hearing boasting about the scenery up here, but honestly, I can't help it—It's all I say it is! Of all the people, I know that you and Doc, who are real nature lovers too, can particularily picture the beauties of this country.*

*You know there is a little deer mouse living with me in my tent. He must run a mouse saloon or night club, because he prefers late hours. I never see him during the daytime, only the evenings. He is a cute little jigger with his big, round ears and beady eyes. He's a clean little rascal, too. His chest and belly is as white as snow as compare with his sleek gray coat of hair. He's as quick as a flash. I have a burlap bag for a rug in front of my cot. A few minutes ago "Eich-haus," that's what I call him was running around here absolutely unafraid of me. For a minute he sat up on that rug on his haunches about 3 feet from where I am sitting, and he "washed his face" with his fore-paws. I have to laugh at him. Next to the head end of my cot I have my barracks bag. On it I used to always keep a couple of candy bars from the P.X., but I had to discontinue that practise, because "Eich-haus" would get into them no sooner than I turned out the light and got into bed. Now I keep one bar only there for him—that's his! Almost every nite just after I get in my "fart sack" I have to snicker, because there he is crinkling the cellophane wrapper on the candy bar, eating chocolate. I guess he thinks he's putting one over on me; he doesn't know that the whole bar is his!*

*I helped work on a lay-out sketch a few days ago for a barracks up here. You can imagine what that means for certain.*

*I maybe shouldn't say this, lest you jump at conclussions that may result in bitter disapointment, but today the members of the outfit I am camped near, all had to report whether in the Eastern or Western half of the states. Maybe some action being taken on possible furloughs. Could be! Keep your fingers crrossed for me! If so, I imagine will be well into Winter before any action is taken though. Yet, it sure sounds good!*

Seen in winter, this pile bridge over the Liard River was 1270 ft. long, took nine days to build, and was finished on the same day troops met at Contact Creek.

119

## MORE SNAPSHOTS FROM A SOLDIER'S SCRAPBOOK

Muncho Lake... from the cliff-top road vantage point.

The 1400 ft. Liard River crossing... a hive of activity.

Chow Line.                                        Mail call.

A D-8 "Cat" crosses the Coal River bridge.

On the move... breaking camp.

Sgt. Halfacre studies aerial photos.

Hunt, Forziati and Gras.

# CHAPTER XI

# PROSPECTS OF ANOTHER WINTER...

**Extracts From Sid Navratil's Diaries**

*October 4, 1942          Sunday          On the Liard*

*"Indian Summer" is at an end. Overcast sky and a westerly wind that whips the rain drops against the canvas bring tidings of a winter, a hard winter, in which poor Southerners are completely out of place. The sleeping bag is no longer "too warm" at night.*

*I'm back at portraiture, and have been asked by Master Sgt. Kuppe to do a series of sketches illustrating the history of the outfit. There isn't much time for it, tho, as days are short and there is no light in our tents. I hope to do most of it back in the States.  Old Man (Trigger) Eschbach left us, to be attached in Texas. We may all go there after this job is finished.*

*October 21, 1942          Wednesday*

*Our surveying parties are completing the survey which was brought up to Watson Lake—and it's high time, too, as there is snow on the ground, now there to stay. The birches are bare again, and the evergreens loaded to the limit with the white flakes. There must be an entire family of ermine in the camp, as we saw two running through our kitchen tent. Their fur is spotless white, tipped black at the end of tail.*

*In the small settlement here at Lower Post we've been buying the two stores out.  The most popular items are the moccasins, and the*

Sgt. Chris Gras - Watson Lake sign post.

*Indian squaws were kept busy until they ran out of moose hide. I managed two pair, one for myself and one to take home.*

*It's almost a certainty that we're going to stay up here in this country over the winter. There is a promise of a furlough, and needless to say we need it pretty badly.*

*In four days we're "moving out"; beginning what should be a very long ride back to Fort Nelson. Where to from Fort*

Hudson's Bay store - Lower Post.

*Nelson, only the future will tell. They're saying Fort Simpson; one of our parties has already started surveying a road to that cold outpost in the Northwest Territories.*

*October 29, 1942          Thursday*

*We have been promised emergency barracks, a dining hall and a recreation hall for our stay here this winter. The question of a furlough is still uncertain, but the chances are good. There is plenty of reading material in the PX, and so the future is not too glum. I've sent home for more supplies, knowing that I'll have plenty of time for sketching.*

*What we will do here during the winter months is still unknown. Most probably we'll drive trucks over the icy road, a rather unpleasant prospect. Oh well...*

*November 1, 1942          Sunday          Camp at Liard Crossing*

*The tents are up and construction of a permanent camp has begun. Six inches of snow, coming after a severe blizzard, announces that we are finally snowbound for the winter.*

Base Camp - Liard River Crossing and prospect of another winter...

*November 7, 1942*       *Saturday*       *Base Camp, Liard River Crossing, BC, Canada*

      *A bitter winter has set in. In the wake of a blizzard that shook our tents as tho they were paper houses, the frost came, bringing the thermometer way down to 15 below. The little stove is red hot in the evenings, but the radius of heat is only a few feet; so we crowd around it, roasting our fronts and freezing our backs. The nights are worse. Crawling into the frozen bag (the accumulated moisture in the eider-down freezes too!) is almost an agony; every inch of exposed flesh freezes over, making one crawl way deep inside, only to come up for air again, and in spite of the double feather coverings, our bones ache in the mornings. The mornings are not so bad except when it comes to one's turn to build the fire at the first whistle. The second, the chow whistle, brings us all out—and sometimes even that doesn't do the trick—as we rush out to the cold chow line. A cloud of steam is coming from the open kitchen tent as we slowly advance, holding the frozen mess kits. It's funny, but we kinda wish for the hot days of gnats and mosquitoes.*

      *The construction of our permanent barracks has begun with the building of the kitchen. The cooks and the KP's (us) need it above everything else as it is no easy task to scrub the pots and pans when the water freezes over as soon as it hits the metal. There is a shortage of building materials, and our sergeant has to go around stealing nails from other outfits. When our prefabricated barracks are up, we hope to have a certain amount of comfort. A sort of a latrine has just been completed, replacing the trench in the woods.*

      *A "wood detail" is busy all day long sawing wood for the stoves. The men's cheeks have that frost-bitten glow. One can't stand still outside.*

      *The lucky few of us in the operations tent still have enough to do to keep us busy for a few more weeks. On the side and in our spare moments we all designed emblems for our Command—the North Western Service Command to which we are now attached. The insignia will go on our sleeves when—and if—we get our furloughs in the future. This favorite subject of conversation has gradually lessened, and now it's almost a taboo even to mention it. The candlelight that casts a very meager light on the paper is tiring my eyes.*

*November 9, 1942*       *Monday*

      *A continuous snow fall has been steadily transforming this country into a winter wonderland. The days are filled with the sounds of hammers, saws, and the trucks as the work on our barracks continues. At noon all the chimneys throw out billows of smoke that mixes lazily with the falling flakes. Sometimes the sun tries weakly to penetrate the clouds, and at that moment it always appears to be morning as its orbit is very low. The other day I was able to observe and photograph an unusual sight—a snow-bow. Instead of an arc, there was only a vertical shaft of rainbow colors that hovered at the foot of the nearest mountain. It couldn't have been more than 1000-feet away from me as I pointed the movie camera at it. A fine spray of snow that was coming practically out of nowhere (as the skies were clear) must have been the reason for this sight.*

*November 16, 1942        Monday*

*A wind of tornado proportions crashed through the giant birches that seem to bend down to their roots. A hazy moon is trying to penetrate the snow dust that whirls through the air, entering the tents and sending cold showers into our faces. The center pole sways precariously and the stove pipe squeaks helplessly as the gale rages on. It's going to be a hard winter all right, but we have one promise to warm our hearts: the furloughs are coming out, definitely!*

*November 17, 1942        Tuesday*

*Icy blasts that seem to go thru one's bones, kept us shivering all day long. Wood-cutting is the occupation now...*

## LIFE IN CAMP

About a mile from the Liard crossing we built a mess hall and set up a Quonset hut. We also dug a deep four-hole latrine. It began to snow and got very cold. It was then our problem with the latrine began. It began filling up, forming columns all the way up to the holes. We couldn't use it because we might become high-centered.

The captain had me and two other men build a fire in the latrine. I told Daunhauer and Warren to get a little gasoline and start a fire. They poured about five gallons of gasoline down a hole, and then, for some reason, proceeded to wait.

Finally, they threw in a lighted match, and the latrine exploded, plastering the sides and roof with a brown substance and toilet paper, which immediately froze. It looked like some bizarre kind of Christmas decorations. Daunhauer and Warren had their eyebrows burned off, and were a mess. We did use the latrine afterwards, but I sure wouldn't have wanted to be there when it warmed up in the spring.

Chris Gras

125

# WINTERS WERE TOUGH!

In our double layer sleeping bag, clothes were placed between the inner and outer layers. When you crawled into the bag, it was so cold that your body would contract into a ball at the upper end of the bag. You would then kick out one leg further down and it was so cold you would immediately bring it back. This warming up procedure would go on until you would reach the end of the bag. By that time you are exhausted and fall off to sleep.

In the morning there is a sheet of ice on your chest which had built up from your breath condensing on the cold outer surface of the sleeping bag. You cross your arms under your chin and break the ice from the sleeping bag. The tent was always white due to the frozen condensation on the inside of the canvas.

The clothes that you placed between the layers of the sleeping bag liners will be warm when put on in the morning. When putting on your boots, you can tell how cold the temperature is by the number of eyelets that can be laced before the fingers can no longer hold the shoelace. After you warm your hands under your armpits, you can continue the lacing of the boots.

Each tent has a potbellied stove that is started by turns by each occupant of the tent. Usually in the evening, when the tent is still warm, the kindling is prepared, with paper and the thinnest strips of wood on the bottom; then comes the thicker wood, until a kind of a pyramid is created. That is then stashed very carefully outside of the stove until morning when the stove is again colder than a grave. Right after the first whistle, the "fire-tender" rushes to the cold stove, rattles the grate once or twice, shoves in the kindling and lights it. This procedure usually takes about 40 seconds, after which the fire-tender rushes back into the still warm sack.

At breakfast-time, you can't even see the mess tent because of the clouds of steam that surround it. You grope around inside until someone plops something in your mess-kit. By the time you reach your tent, the food is a frozen blob which you immediately plunge into the hot stove to thaw it out. The slice of bread that had been sawed from the frozen loaf in the mess tent by the cooks earlier, is then placed, resting on a coat-hanger, against the red-hot side of the Sibley stove, making toast fit for a king.

The only heat in the tent comes from the stove, so the part of the body facing it is warm, the other side is freezing. The way the Indians tell it, "White man dumb; build big fire in front, freeze in back. Indian is smart; builds two small fires, one in front, one in back. Freeze all over."

Normally the temperature is twenty or thirty below. Then all of a sudden, the temperature rises. The snow and ice is starting to melt, and before you know it, water is running freely all over the area. It's the Chinook, and the air is warm like a beautiful spring day, lasting for several hours. Suddenly the temperature again falls, everything instantly freezes and you are back in the normal twenty-to-thirty-below zero environment.

Stanley Caldwell

**Extracts from Sid Navratil's Diaries**

Saturday                                    Nov. 28, 1942

The new huts afford us such luxuries as writing & reading atop our beds in our shirtsleeves, sleeping in comparative comfort and on the whole living more like civilized beings. In the evening there is usually much going on: card playing and open discussions of all sorts. One even looks forward to these evenings when he gets a chance to plan & discuss the plans for the future.

Thanksgiving Day we went swimming in nearby sulphur springs. The air was crisp — about -5° — and the pool sent clouds of steam into the air. The surrounding shrubs and trees were white with thick frost — the entire scene seemed unreal as we swam in the hot (100°F) water. Those were agonizing moments as we dried ourselves before the fire, our bodies steaming as tho they were afire. Up to then the slogan was, "Cleanliness is Next to Impossible;" that is changed now.

My turn for furlough is 25th in line, and as the first bunch hasn't left yet, I can't expect to be home before Christmas. Perhaps in January.

## THANKJGIVING DAY LIARD HOTJPRINGJ JWIM

Last one in's a rotten egg...

Weidman lathers up.

Enchanted surroundings for a Thanksgiving day swim.

*December 14, 1942        Monday*

There is so much snow that the huts look like huge white mounds. It feels good to walk in it, breathing in that damp air with its crystal stars.

The mail call was a pleasant one, too, today. Almost everyone carried away a package or two.

The day of our departure is not known yet; so much speculation is always going on. The conviction that we'll get 30 days of furlough upon reaching the States is so strong that should we get only 15 there will be much complaining. The possibility of no leave at all is not even considered.

Caldwell in a Nissan hut by a Sibley stove

*December 16, 1942        Wednesday*

Two feet of snow are being whipped by a strong wind. The camp looks like a movie blizzard scene. The wind knocks the breath out and makes one stagger. But—everyone's happy. Cases are packed and as soon as our trucks are repaired, we're off for home.

*December 18, 1942        Saturday*

Sid Navratil - Liard camp.

Our days in Canada are drawing to a close. The "Operations" equipment and books were crated and shipped away today, and our own barracks bags are filled to capacity—and waiting. The camp to which we're going is known to everyone now: Camp McCoy, Wisconsin, a cold, windy place on Lake Michigan. We're well acclimated, though, and won't mind. The "main thing"—as Carl would say—is that we'll be in our own States. After company reorganization, we will probably go out again, either to Australia where the rest of our battalion is stationed or to Nicaragua, where the Pan-American road is being built. Or we may go to any other of thousands of possible places.

129

*Early tomorrow morning we're going to start our 500-mile trip to Fort St. John, B.C. The road, packed firmly with much snow, promises to give us a rough travel. However, the ride, as compared to our arrival (at Ft. Nelson) last winter, is going to be in comfort as we'll ride in the closed "carry-alls," My camera is loaded, and I'm hoping to have a sunny day; it's going to be the next-to-shortest day in the year, and this far north, the days are about five hours long.*

Winter view of Steamboat Mountain on our trip out of the north.

*December 23, 1942        Wednesday        Dawson Creek, B.C. (Railhead)*

*Five hundred miles of cold road is behind us, and a day or two after Xmas we'll be on the train going home. Just now I'm bothered by a deuce of a cold caught during the trip.*

*Tomorrow, 24th, I'm KP in our new "casual" camp, "breaking in" the new kitchen. Yet the thought that we're going home is going to make this a happy Christmas for me. I keep humming "Goin' Home." It's cold as the devil (-26 F) but the nights are beautiful, sure to leave an indelible impression on my mind.*

*Everyone is drinking beer and feeling quite happy...*

*December 24, 1942        Thursday        Christmas Eve*

*The crowded, smoky hut shows no trace of a holiday spirit. But the kitchen in which I spent 15 hours of KP duty today, is busy preparing for the holiday dinner tomorrow. Tonight, after our work was over, we had mail-call, probably our last one in Canada. The letters, all from home and Helen, brought a pang of regret into my heart—I would have given anything to be able to spend this one evening at home. The strains of "Going Home" ran through my mind again—it was the grand chord that ends the finale—and I felt just then as tho I was there, in that familiar circle around the table. Two candles cast a yellow light on the solemn faces as the Lord's*

*Prayer is said. And in that spiritual picture I could even envision Charlie in his shirt sleeves, leading the rest in a prayer—and an "extra" one—for the misguided mankind.*

*Were I to write a letter to "him" now, I would probably say,"Charlie— today, on this great day, in this world is being born something great; in this crazed world is coming into being a Spirit, a Spirit that binds all men into one glorious self. Even a war, or rather, only a war will bring into the man's brain the realization of why He was born. Only by great trials such as this one will man look into his soul to begin to see a flicker of the Light."*

*December 26, 1942      Saturday*

*I spent Christmas Day with a miserable cold. Everyone seemed to think that the proper way of celebrating was by being drunk, and some went to extremes. Someone produced a bottle of 130 proof rum, as vile a drink as can be found in cheapest of dives, which had a knock-out effect on the men who drank it. Chuck showed it most—his eyes were bloodshot as he shouted curses on all of us, calling us "yellow bastards" for being here instead of where there is danger. He has a brother in the Air Corps, serving near Samoa, and his drunken jabber showed how worried he was. He's very young, and usually does not drink.*

*The turkey dinner was fine, except the turkey, that we found out this morning, at about four, when, as if by a command, everyone was getting up to make a dash for the latrine. Some of the fellows failed to make it. This was repeated all day today as we loaded the flat-cars.*

Our gear at the Dawson Creek railhead... bound for the lower 48.

*December 27, 1942        Sunday*

*The change from arctic to "GI" clothing accomplished, we are ready to leave. Spain and I went to "town" for dinner and were very disappointed. Coffee and sugar rationing we found distasteful, beer parlours closed, and so was the movie. It was bitter cold, and we felt the chill through our lighter clothing. And so we hurried back to our comfortable hut.*

*Tomorrow morning at 3 we're to start out on our special train. I hope everything goes well from there on...*

*December 30, 1942        Wednesday        En Route Home*

*The train is speeding through the wheat country—stretches of flat, wind and snow-blown fields. We "pulled out" of Dawson Creek early Monday morning, and some time tonight should again cross the border. It's a gray day, and with the frosted windows shutting off most of the view, the ride is uninteresting.*

*December 31, 1942        Thursday*

*Back in the States again. The train is speeding towards Minneapolis where we will probably change to day coaches that will take us to McCoy.*

*In the middle of our drunken revelry last night (the liquor we bought in Moose Jaw, Sask., into which town we were turned loose for 30 minutes) we were jolted by a crash into our Pullman by a passenger car. The train stopped about a mile or so from the accident.*

# CHAPTER XII

# SIMPSON TRAIL ASSIGNMENT
# HARRY'S LETTERS HOME

*Sunday Afternoon:*
*November 8, 1942*                    *Camp near Fort Nelson, B.C., Canada*

*A small group of us have been detached from our Company, and are now on the verge of another new adventure. We are now temporarily camped in a tent down here near the tiny settlement of Fort Nelson, where we first started from last April. We came down here over the "Alcan Highway" in a heated "carry-all." The journey was over 200 miles from our Company camp, and I enjoyed it immensely, because it was my first glimpse of the finished road. I have never seen scenery on par with it anywhere in all my life. As I sat in our vehicle gazing through the frosty windowpane as we rolled along over this great highway it was like paging thru colored wilderness scenes in a National Geographic magazine. The fresh snowfall over the mountain summits made everything a Winter fairyland. I shall never forget that trip. Now I am certain that some day when the war has finally ceased, all of us are going to take a trip up over this great highway together.*

"Scenic" Alaska Highway - Trout River area.

133

Censorship forbids the disclosure of much information concerning our new mission. Somehow, I am one of those selected by our Commanding Officer. This is to be another road job. I cannot tell you many details, the purpose, the direction or the estimated distance, but I can say that it will pierce thru real wilderness and will end at a remote trappers settlement at a junction of great Arctic rivers. I estimate that we will be out in the "bush" again for 2 months.

On the heels of a real, old-fashioned snowstorm Winter pounced upon this country in earnest about a week ago. About 4 inches of snow cover the ground and the mercury only rises above zero a few degrees during the day light hours. During the wee hours of the night the mercury always takes a toboggan ride. A few nites ago an official 27 degrees below was recorded at the airport near here. The fact that we had such an unusually mild and pleasant Fall and suddenly a cold snap moved in was pretty tough on us for a few days, but already we are adapting ourselves to it. Very fortunately, it is a dry cold up here and the government has equipped us with excellent Arctic clothing. We are all clad in our moccasins, shoe pacs, heavy trousers, parkas and fur hats now. The toughest part of this weather is getting up in the morning in your "long-johns" when it is about 20 degrees below and getting a fire started. Brrr!!!!

Of course, you have probably already surmised that I probably won't be home for the holidays if present plans materialize. You can't feel any sadder about this than I, because all Summer long I have been dreaming about spending Xmas at home with you folks. Such is our fate in a war-torn world. However, in a little talk by our Commanding Officer just before we left our base camp, we fellows were given one consolation and promise. When we tie-in the line on this new job, our party is supposed to get a furlough priority. Furloughs are now official and it is rumoured that they will be 15 days long plus travelling time.

Cost and variety of equipment being mustered for the new expedition seems relatively unimportant. We have been issued the finest in winter clothing and sleeping equipment. We fellows look like real Eskimos when we get all dressed up in our duds. A special ration has been formulated for our party. Plenty of meat and vegetables, flour and fruit will be taken, and each meal will constitute a double ration. About 20 drag horses to pull sleds with horse food and our supplies, and a number of dog teams have been contracted for the trip. Quite a number of local trappers and freighters from up here are going along to keep the outfit moving. Even though sub-zero temperatures and Arctic blizzards are going to prove a menace, if present plans work out, I think we will make it alright. Then too, our party is going to be divided and we are going to relieve each other. This is going to be a "blitz" job and when we reach our destination, we are going to be almost in the "land of the midnight sun." Already we only have about 9 hours of daylight. Just a few days prior to Xmas we should have only a few daylight hours. Every night the Northern Lights present brilliant heavenly displays.

*Last nite I had an enjoyable evening. Six of us went down to the little 12 building settlement of Fort Nelson. We crossed the river on the ice. The little settlement was a pretty site in the dusk of the evening. Wood fires from the snug little cabins covered the valley with a veil of tangy smelling smoke. We browsed around in the Hudson Bay store and then we visited at a little log hut that was a combination general store and Post Office. We stayed there for supper. What a delicious meal we had! We all sat at one big table near a crackling drum stove under a gasoline lantern. There were four trappers and local characters at the table with us. The supper cost us 6 bits apiece, and it certainly was a real treat! I enjoyed the fellowship and the delicious meal equally as well. Mrs George, who cooked the meal, was the first woman I saw since last Spring. She made me a little homesick as I watched her busily bustling around the kitchen preparing supper. It was quite a novelty for us to eat off China plates.*

George's General Store and Post Office (Mr. George at right)

Photo courtesy George Behn.

*All the natives are now using their dog teams up here. Every little cabin in Fort Nelson has a mushing sled standing up against it, and a number of sled dogs tied up. While we were down there last nite 2 teams went dashing by. Those dogs were going lickety-split and they seemed to enjoy their task as they flew past with their tails wagging like ostrich plumes and they yelped and barked. Some of these dog teams sure can travel.*

*Every dog in town was yelping when we left and re-crossed the river on the ice, and then way off in the distance we could hear a low, eiry howl of a pack of wolves. I shall never forget some of the experiences up here.*

*November 17, 1942*          *B.C., Canada*

*We are now working on the new assignment. Considerable progress has already been made, and once more I am deep in the wilderness far from civilization. At present we are working from the head of construction and are camping with the construction unit, but in a few days the party will strike out ahead in earnest when the horses and dog teams have all arrived. You wouldn't believe the amazing speed that a dog team can make over a good trail. 75 miles in a day is not uncommon for a good 5-dog string of huskies and that is pulling a loaded sled! I got a big kick out of watching three teams start down over the frozen river from the settlement about a week ago. I don't have the time to elaborate so many interesting details of my new, recent experiences up here, but if I should get to see you some-time, I sure will be able to spin you some real yarns.*

Baptiste Villeneuve's dogsled team.

*We are having real Winter weather up here. There is a 6-inch blanket of powdery snow on the ground and the average temperature is about zero. When we got up this morning, it was 17 degrees below.*

*November 26, 1942*          *B.C., Canada*
*Thanksgiving Day*

*Since I first started this letter to you over a week has already passed, so you can see how difficult it is for me to find time for correspon-dence. With running line for the road, hustling all our rations, supplies and equipment and frequently moving our camp we have been quite busy. We are now almost ready for the big push. 4 dog teams and 20 drag horses to pull toboggans are here now at our camp. The toboggans are being assem-bled right here at present. About 25 local civilians have been engaged to move the outfit thru. Just think—all these elaborate plans to move all our small surveying party thru! Most of the civilians going with us, a few of them Indians, are real woodsmen. It's a pleasure to watch them work in the bush. We have dandy white wall tents to live in each equipped with a good stove and a brand new Coleman gasoline lantern. This is a big job, and I know it's not going to be a picnic, but if the weather doesn't get too severe, I believe we'll make it thru without too much difficulty.*

*Nothing is being overlooked for comfort and conveyance this trip. Yesterday a couple crates of skis and Siwash snowshoes arrived. This time we're travelling in grand style. If time permitted, I could write pages all about our set-up and about this new job. If we get thru alright this will be another experience I will long remember. Today a medic arrived, who is going along with us too.*

*About half a mile from our present camp there is an Indian village. A few days ago a few of us were over there. Their huskies howled in a chorus and announced our arrival. The few Indians that were outside ran to their cabins when they saw us. No one came out for quite a while but we could see them shyly peeping thru the windows at us. Finally one Indian came out that could speak some English and soon we were invited into his snug log cabin. The rather modern conveniences they have and their apparent cleanliness amazed me. This group of Indians seems both prosperous and progressive. Some of the fellows bought a few shaggy looking pelts at the village. I bought 2 pair of moose-hide moccasins to wear this Winter.*

*Well folks, just as in a meal, the dessert, the best part of the spread is left to the last, so with this letter. Here is the big news! Furloughs are now official and in order. Our party has furlough priority. At the completion of this mission our survey party is supposed to be sent home in a group. Our Captain was down here a few days ago and with Colonel's sanction, broke the good news to us. Furlough plans at present call for 15 days at home plus travelling time.*

SIMPSON Trail

Toleson - Ludwich - Stevenson

"To furnish volunteer aid to the sick and wounded of armies..." and "To act in matters of voluntary relief and in accord with the military and naval authorities as a medium of communication between the people of the United States of America and their Army and Navy..." The Charter of the American National Red Cross. By Act of Congress, January 5, 1905.

Cartoon by Cpl. Blackmon - on Red Cross stationary.

*November 28, 1942*                    *British Columbia, Canada*

*To my surprise we had a swell Thanksgiving spread up here. Three turkeys were sent out from the Q.M. with all the trimmings. The cooks did a swell job on the birds. During the afternoon I went over and helped them. I put on a white apron and we made a dressing and stuffed the plump birds. While they were roasting we made a big batch of doughnuts. A cook mixed the dough and rolled it out on top of a ration crate with a beer bottle and cut them out. I heated them in the grease and fried them. We had a whole cardboard box full when we were finished.*

*In our tent another lad and I set up some ration boxes and made a large table and seats. The tablecloth large bright red strip of our surveyor's signal cloth. We got out the officers mess chest and we ate from plates instead of our G.I. mess gear. Just before we ate, we all sat down and our lieutenant said a few appropriate words about Thanksgiving and our being away from our loved ones and he read a prayer.*

*A whole turkey was on the table, golden brown, on a big platter. By golly, no one in the group knew how to carve one. I was elected. Thanks to watching Doc wield the expert carving knife on so many elegant fowl at home, I did a pretty good job if I do say so myself.*

*All in all, I enjoyed our Thanksgiving celebration first rate.*

*I wish you could see our dog teams. I get a kick out of these hunts.*

*By golly, they sure can "haul the mail." These huskies are real contortionists. I have seen them racing along pulling a loaded sled down the trail with their bells a jingling as they barked and yelped, and the lead dog would suddenly swerve off the trail towards a stump, and as he passed it like a flash hoist his leg and dash on. In the rhythmic sequence every dog in the string followed suit! Not one flinches. Boy, I get a big laugh when I see them. Those pooches got the trick down pat.*

*Christmas Eve*                       *Muskwa, B.C. Canada*
*December 24, 1942*

*A year ago to this evening about dusk I arrived at Camp Claiborne, La. In the interim so much has happened and I have had so many unusual and exciting experiences, joys, sorrows, and disappointments that I find it difficult to recollect all these occurrences. Here it is a cold Arctic nite and truly a "white Xmas." By candle light in a warm, winterized tent, 2 companions and I are seated about a rough table writing these letters to our folks.*

*It being Christmas, my heart is not heavy, but my thoughts are constantly with you and I long to be at home with you.*

*Well the job that I told you about in my last letter is now history and rather a rugged memory. If I had any linguistic talent, I could write a book of my past month's experiences that would be on par with Jack London's tales of the Northland. Brevity prohibits a detailed account here, but here are a few high spots. 3 of us hit the field and relieved 3 of our colleagues that were "running the line." The outfit consisted of 20 horses, 20 toboggans, 25 civilians and 5 dog teams. We had quite a nice camp set-up, and this outfit moved with us each day. We had a new home each nite. Although the temperature always well below zero, fortunately it was not rough. We managed to live fairly comfortable, and we enjoyed the good chow that 2 cooks prepared under difficulties.*

*Do you recall the pontoon plane that I mentioned flying during the Summer? Well, that same plane equipped with wheels and landing gear flown by Mac, the same pilot, contacted us almost daily. Our course was guided by the plane from which we gained our compass bearings. When we used to hear the drone of the Norseman" we would quickly light a fire and the pilot would locate our position by the column of smoke. When he spotted us he would signal us by dipping or "wiggling" his wings and circling us. Quite often he would swoop down over us and drop messages to us from our lieutenant which were contained in a sealed can with a long red streamer attached to it. Whenever messages were dropped, it was quite a thrill, because Mac would roar over us so low that once he brushed the snow off the crown of a spruce tree with a wheel of the plane. Old McPhie sure can make that plane of his talk!*

*One day the plane came over and dropped a message stating that they were going to land on a lake that we had just passed, back to which*

McPhie's Norseman "taxi" on Simpson Trail mission.

*2 dog mushers, 2 dog teams and one of my buddies and I were to return. We were met by our lieutenant. To my surprise, I was put in charge of the group and we loaded all of our equipment into the plane. With 7 passengers, our tonnage, 2 dog sleds and 9 huskies, we were crammed in like sardines. With a roar and an artificial snowstorm behind us, Mac lifted us off the lake and we were off. For a few minutes the dogs were quarrelsome, but once in the air they were just as meek as lambs. Some of the pooches enjoyed a trip, and kept looking out of the windows as we floated over the stretches of Godforsaken wilderness. One of the dogs got airsick and heaved almost in my lap. What a stench! I started to get woozy feeling myself. As dusk approached, we landed on a large silent lake. Out outfit was quickly unloaded, I received my instructions from the lieutenant and the plane again took off and I watched it's tail light fade into the darkness, and then gazed into the dark, deep silence, I sure felt lonely. We hitched up the dogs and mushed to shore, where in the dark we set up our camp. I was pretty disgusted because we were given a tent with a hole burned in it, and contrary to what we were informed our cooking outfit was a blamed poor one. We had to make a pot out of empty large tin cans which we had emptied. I was pretty hot about the poor outfit they sent us out with. The one dog musher with us was a Cree Indian. I sure was glad he was along, because he sure was handy, and a real trails man. He is a trapper up here but a forest fire ruined a good share of his line so he took a job on our outfit.*

*My buddy and I had about 30 miles of line to blaze. We had one river to cross and were to tie in at another large lake, where another party of our boys headed to from another direction. After 8 days of weary battling the line over incredible windfall, rough muskeg, open swamp areas, spruce so thick a dog couldn't get thru, and cussed miles of alders so thick that at times we had to crawl thru, we finally tied in at our destination, and almost hit it on the nose. I never went thru such a miserable country in all my life! Of course making our own camp, and cooking our own meals after a hard*

*3:00 PM.*
*You ARE 3 m:*
*from*
*Dog Lake*
*Give er Hell*

Dec. 22, 1942

MEMORANDUM TO:

Corps. Spiegel and Blackmon;

Sgt. Tolleson and Stevenson went in to Nelson this afternoon yesterday evening. I am anxiously hoping that you will tie to his line at Dog Lake to-day, so that we may get you in. I am aware of the good job you are doing and of the tough conditions under which you are working.

Dog Lake lies between 5 and 6 miles from the river x-ing of Popular River.

I am afraid that Tolleson did not put a flag out on the lake when he ended his line, so it may be necessary to search closely for it. The plane will pull you to the West end of Dog Lake with your line. At this end of the lake and out on the lake, is a cache of rations. This cache is marked by a spruce tree, cut and set up out on the lake on the ice. You will have no difficulty recognizing the cache, as it is marked precisely the same as was the cache on Big Lake that you took off from. Somewhere a short distance back from the shore line, at the Western End of the lake, and in the vicinity of the cache, Tolleson stopped his line and came to the plane. They were not with their dog teams. If you can pick up the tracks of two men, not with dogs, leading from the vicinity of cache to shore line, they will doubtless lead you to the line. They were the only ones who walked from the shore, not with the dogs.

I will enclose a rather poor sketch, I hope that it may be of some help.

What is the trouble with the dog teams? I can't understand why they can't keep camp up to the head of the line.

Your line last night was in the vicinity of Popular River x-ing, your camp 1½ mi from Popular River. If you make Dog Lake to-day it will mean approx. 7½ mi. of walking, between 5 and 6 of which you will have to blaze. However the going isn't so very tough, and it may be quite possible you will make it. The plane will work right on until dark, weather permitting, and, if weather permits, and you make Dog Lake, will fly the outfit into Nelson by moonlight.

Good Luck

Lancaster

Lt. Lancaster's air dropped message.

*days work wasn't exactly a picnic. Weight being an important item, we were limited to a monotonous diet of bacon, bannock, dehydrated spuds, rice, tea, and dried fruit. By the way, I'm quite an accomplished bannock baker, now.*

*Of course almost daily we were contacted by the plane, guided and dropped messages. On the last day we struck pretty decent country and we kept on working a few hours after dark. I ran the compass all the way and*

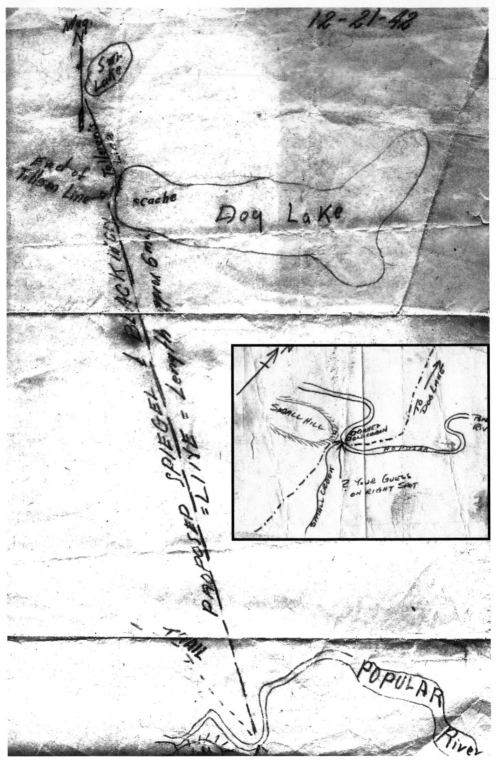

Lt. Lancaster's hand-drawn maps - air dropped to Spiegel and Blackmon.

my partner blazed the line behind me. After dark I took my shots while my partners held a flashlight on the instrument. Bewiskered, tired, dirty, and hungry we finally tied in about 7:00pm on the shortest day of the year. Happy that our assignment was completed, we found an expected cache of food on the lake and we were just about to pick up our campsite and pre-pare a real feed for ourselves, when we heard the moan of a plane. It was Mac coming for us! We blinked our flashlight and he signalled with his landing lights. He landed on the lake as graceful as a bird, and what a reunion we had! We loaded on, and after 3 attempts at a take-off, once more were aloft. We flew up to a settlement at the Northern terminus of our line and landed. There I saw the mighty, ice-locked MacKenzie River for the first time in my life. Our lieutenant was anxiously awaiting our arrival. He was so happy to see us, he couldn't do enough for us. As tattered, torn and dirty as I was he introduced me to a number of "big-shots" in the officer's quarters and told them all about our trip. I guess he was proud of us.

That nite we bunked in pretty nifty big log cabins where the pilots and air corps men stay. At dawn the next morning we took off in the plane again and after a wonderful 2-hour flight we arrived back at our starting point again. From the air we could see our line running thru the wilderness just like a string stretched across a topographical map. We spotted a number of herds of caribou, and some moose. One big bull was charging thru the bush, because the roar of the plane frightened him. The flight back certainly was wonderful.

From here on this letter isn't going to be so pleasant, because I have bad news to import. When we arrived back here at the airport we found out that we are orphans. Our whole company, save the 12 of us, have left and are reported headed back to the States. They cleared out a few days prior to our return. 2 lieutenants were left with us, too. We haven't found out any details yet, but it is rumoured that we are to be transferred to the construction unit up here as a permanent road location outfit, and also that another job is awaiting us pronto. All of us, including our officers are angry, because it appears that we were wilfully lied to and deceived into believing that we would be issued furloughs at the completion of this mission. If we are transferred to this other outfit, it's going to be a tough break for we fellows, because it's mighty difficult to get any place in a well set-up organization. So far we can't find out anything about the future of our company. I don't know, but we may get furloughs yet, but things look rather dark for us right now. If we don't, we certainly will be getting a raw deal. What complicates matters even more is that our outfit moved out with 2 months of our pay. Some of our boys are broke now. I'm a little more fortunate, because I still have over 60 berries in my wallet yet.

Well, it's an ill wind, that blows no good so we may get a break yet, and these recent developments, although disappointing may prove to be a blessing in disguise. Until we get more dope on our plight, I'm going to keep my fingers crossed and hope for the best.

*At present we are staying at the airport here, and chowing in the air corps. mess hall. These boys are swell chaps, and we are eating like kings. Tomorrow, they are going to have a real Xmas turkey dinner, followed by a moving picture show entitled "Rise and Shine" followed by a beer-bust. We have been invited to this celebration and I am anxiously looking forward to it. This will be the first movie I have seen in almost a year.*

*P.S. Enclosed is a few sample message sheets that were dropped from the plane on our location job.*

*Saturday Afternoon:*
*December 26, 1942*          *Muskwa, B.C. Canada*

*My Dear brother, gosh, it sure seems good. This morning we slept in until almost noon. That's one thing about our group—we sure are an independent bunch of fellows. Was down to the settlement and saw some of the trappers that worked for us packing last summer and dog mushers on this last trip. We had quite a reunion and it being the festive season, bottles of rum were passed freely. That stuff sure is "mighty potent."*

*Well Christmas day I also received another pleasant surprise. I received an envelope from my Commanding Officer which contained a statement of promotion. On Dec. 22nd I was officially promoted from Cpl. Technician to the grade of Sergeant Technician or a T4. With our 20% for foreign service, I will now net almost 94 berries in American mazuma. Naturally, I am pleased with this promotion, but as I stated in my letter home, if we "orphans" are adopted by an organization that is already set up, we may lose all our ratings and be back down to buck-ass privates again. That would be a tough break, all right. We fellows all have our fingers crossed.*

*P.S.- 43 degrees below zero here last nite.*

*December 30, 1942*          *Muskwa, B.C., Canada*

*We are still "shacked up" here at the airport, and for the present, not doing much but laying low, resting and eating 3 good square meals a day. Of course, the issue uppermost in all of our minds is furloughs. The situation still looks favourable, but still no official confirmation. At present, we are awaiting a radiogram from our superiors on the issue, which will be the verdict. Awaiting this news is like awaiting the return of the jury in the courtroom, when one's case is being tried.*

*Tomorrow night is New Year's Eve. I will be thinking of all of you at the "shindig" at our house. I too will be celebrating tomorrow night, and doing my bit to "ring out the old and ring in the new" way up here in the bush. Our location party that worked on the last road job is now invited down to a New Year's Eve Party down at Fort Nelson. Many of the horse wranglers and dog mushers that worked with us out there live at the*

Greetings...

from The Alaska Highway
in Northern Canada

Oh! I guess we'll have a turkey,
Christmas dinner, so they say,
Fruit and nuts and cake and candy
We'll enjoy it in a way,
But 'twill be, for all our efforts,
A pretty lonesome day;
Christmas just won't seem like Christmas
With you all so far away.

Xmas Eve 1942

My thoughts are with you tonight. Love, Harry.

settlement. They are rough-cut diamonds, but all swell fellows. This promises to be a wild shindig, as they announced the arrival of many "crocks" of rum in recent plane arrivals from the "outside." Don't worry folks, I'll have probably the best time of all, and Bromo Seltzer and aspirin won't constitute my breakfast the following morning either. Square dancing to the tunes of a guitar and a hill-billy fiddler will be the main attraction of the party. These folks up here go for square dancing and "step dancing" in a big way. The gals down at Nelson sure will be twirled to the wail of the fiddle tomorrow nite!

Hoping to see you all before long,
Love, Harry

P.S. Sgt. Spiegel to you, Bowser.

[Editor's note—In letters home, "Doc" was Harry's father Herman, "Bowser" was his brother, Cpl Carl Spiegel stationed at Key Field Air Squadron, Mississippi.]

# CHAPTER XIII

# CANOL PROJECT STORIES

*Tuesday Afternoon:*
*January 5, 1943*            *Fort St. John, B.C.,*

    *I am dropping you these few lines in haste to let you in on some great news. From the heading on this letter you will notice we are back down at Fort St. John, which was our starting point into the wilderness last Spring.*

    *At present we are checking in our supplies, and awaiting our furlough papers to be issued to us. If all goes according to plan, these papers should be ready shortly and we'll be heading for the "end of steel" at Dawson Creek in a day or so. Except a possible lay over of a day or so there, to be issued some "go to meetin" clothes, to cash Money Orders, purchase railroad tickets, etc., I am being allowed a five day one way to reach Buffalo, once I board the train at Dawson Creek. Present plans provide for 15 full days actually at home + 10 days round trip travel time = 25 days total.*

    *We received our belated pay, so now I have plenty of money for the journey.*

    *Although this furlough situation looks very favorable now, please do not make any plans, lest we all be disappointed. This is the army, and anything can happen. I suggest that you don't mention my pending visit to everyone. Please don't go to any trouble or fuss, and remember, nix on any parties! If I do get home for a while I just want to be with you and enjoy the comforts of home.*

    *Had my first shower bath since I left Louisiana, yesterday. I feel like a "city-slicker" in these nice clean clothes. Sure feels great!*

*[Editor's note—The members of "A" Company - 648th Topo Battalion that had been assigned to the Simpson Trail Project did at last recieve their much covetted furloughs home. Upon completion of their furlough, one officer and a dozen men were ordered to return to Dawson Creek early Febuary 1943.]*

*Saturday Afternoon:*
*February 13, 1943*                    *Fort Alcan, BC  Canada*

*After reading my last letter you are probably a bit puzzled that the heading is still Fort Alcan on this letter. Since I last wrote, a few of our group have been on a regular merry-go-round. With sealed and secret orders and all our army records our group boarded a greyhound bus here and headed for the "end of steel" at Dawson Creek a few days ago. We were ordered to report back to our Company in the States. I told you where they were temporarily stationed when I was at home.*

*Acting as my Lieutenants right hand man, I was kept busy as a bee down there at Dawson, turning in all our Arctic clothing at the Q.M. and getting credit for it, obtaining travel orders for our group, turning in our baggage at the station for shipment and purchasing the Pullman accommodations on behalf of Uncle Sam for our trip back. That evening I had just finished tending to details, and was just going to slide into my sleeping bag and, planning to get up early the next morning to board that 5:30 train out of the bush, when a wire arrived from higher authority to hold our group for further orders. After waiting around for 1 day, another wire was received stating that one officer and four men out of our group were to remain and report back to Fort Alcan. After a pow-wow, it was decided that the following fellows were to head back into the bush: Lt. Lancaster, Sgt. Halfacre (Mitch), "Arky" Tolleson (Oregon), Steve Stephenson (Forest-Service-California) and myself.*

*I have bid farewell to a lot of fine fellows since I'm in the army, but never has it been more difficult to say "good-bye" to a bunch of fellows as when I saw the 8 pals of mine off at the train early that morning. They felt bad that they had to leave us, but were happy with the prospects of returning to the states! I stayed in their car and chatted with them until the whistle blew and the train began to roll. Amidst a hail of good-byes and best wishes, I stepped off the step of the platform. I'm not ashamed to say that my eyes were moist as I stood there alone in the pitch dark of the early morning and watched the lights of the last car fade into darkness.*

*I have one consolation: the 4 fellows I'm still with are the swellest eggs I ever met, and we're all real buddies to the core! We'll tough it out together somehow!*

*Boy, the night before the fellows left Dawson what a celebration we had! Lt. Lancaster was one of us and he spent money as if it was hay! We kept circulating in a cycle from the cafes, restaurants, poolroom, movie and the beer parlor. All that day and at night I averaged a full course dinner all the way from soup or a cocktail to pie and coffee about every three hours. I ate four complete meals that day and the snacks in between. I had my share of beer too, but I knew when to quit. We all sat around one big table in the old-fashioned saloon. What a shindig we had! Of course, we again met some trappers and freighters we had worked with here in the "bush. At* one time there must have been 20 quart bottles of Lager beer bottles on our table. Some of these fellows sure spend money lavishly.

You remember Keenan, the fellow I introduced you to in N.Y.C. Depot? Well, he got to feeling pretty good in the saloon, and he made a friendly bet with a big, bewiskered local character for $2.00. Someone withdrew a set of galloping dominoes from his pocket, and Keenan and this fellow rolled for a point. Keenan won, but the other fellow refused to pay off, accusing him of crooked roll. He challenged Keenan to a fight. They both stripped off their coats. I grabbed my coat and scooted towards the door. Everybody in the place stood up. They went at it and after a few blows, Keenan backed this fellow up against the bar and gave him a hook to the chin. He went down like a chunk of lead. As I disappeared out of the door unseen by my companions, lest I be arrested in the place by the M.P.'s, the fellow was flat on his back stretched out in front of the bar on the floor. I waited around outside on the street and in a few minutes out came the gang—with the $2.00! Immediately we trotted to a restaurant and ordered up again! Nobody has any respect for the value of money in these boom-towns, and the business places are coining money like a mint!

Of course, bootleggers circulate in these towns too, always glad to relieve a soldier of his hard-earned cash. A couple of crocks were bought by our boys—26 dollars for 52 ounces! Wow!! No thank you, again I had no part in that. In all that celebration, I only bought 2 meals for myself; the others wouldn't give me a chance to spend any money!

What big heads some of the boys had the following morning. They couldn't drink enough water to put out the fire.

Well the five of us came back here to Fort Alcan again. Yesterday, I was sent down to Dawson again to redraw Arctic clothing for us. They issued me all new garments this time.

This may sound almost dramatic, but our Lieutenant just came in a few minutes ago, saying that he just received a wire stating that we are to stand by again until further orders. What a mix-up! We were supposed to start from here tomorrow morning for a big, road location job somewhere up in the Yukon and Northwest Territories. We don't know exactly what's up now. Who knows we may go back to the outfit yet! In the army, a man's fate sure dangles on a thread. I will let you know what developments take place.

When we were first to leave here, we were given $12.00 (American) in cash to pay for our meals in the diner on the trip back. Of course we five had to give this back up here yesterday. We received a receipt for it. I was paid a few days ago; I already had about $50.00 set aside to send you, but I am going to keep this for a few days yet until I find out what our next move will be.

> So Long,
> Love, Harry

*Sunday Evening:*
*February 21, 1943*                    *Camp in Teslin Lake, Yukon Territory*

*I certainly have had a wonderful trip up over a 100 mile stretch of the Alcan Highway since I last wrote you. The weather has been incredibly beautiful for this time of year up here, and the highway was in good shape for winter travel, so in spite of cannon-balling a load of freight in a big G.I. cargo truck, the trip was a very pleasant one. We travelled only during daylight hours, and in easy stages. We arrived this afternoon, six days enroute. We are now well into the Yukon Territory, and about to start our new mission from here to the northeast. This job ties into the "Black Gold" job that I told you about when I was home.*

*What beautiful scenery I have seen in the last week! The breathtaking, mountainous terrain through the Canadian Rockies in which I have worked last summer particularly impressed me. From Lower Post northward this is all new country to me, and I certainly am giving my eyes a treat. What marvellous, remote, wilderness country lies up here. As I gaze upon God's handi-work as I pass through, again and again I keep saying to myself "if only you folks could share this scenery with me."*

*My biggest ambition in life now is that all of us will be able to come up through this country together on a camping trip all the way to Alaska when the war is over. I'll show you scenery that will hold you speechless!*

*Wednesday Evening*
*February 24, 1943*                    *Camp on Teslin Lake, Yukon Territory*

*A couple of days ago, Jim and I went with a Major down to the settlement at the other end of Telsin Lake. We went to try to arrange to contract a couple of dog teams for a pending location job. What a remote settlement it is. All the buildings are made out of logs squatted on a fairly open flat over looking the beautiful Lake.*

*I learned a lot about these people from the Mountie, at whose cabin we visited for about an hour. He is a fine, hospitable fellow. I wish you could see the snug little cabin he lives in! Sure is a dandy. I hope to build and live in one like it someday. Wes studied the maps on his wall as he explained the country that we are to pass through to us. Sounds like a rugged go to me. This Mountie was most interesting to listen to, because he has been stationed up at Dawson City, Circle City on the Arctic Circle, and some other remote posts during his career. All this seems like the events of a Northland storybook come true to me.*

*This great network of highways is going to change the lives of the native people, who until now were cut off from the outside world almost completely, a great deal. I sometimes wonder if they would not have been happier and better off if they had remained cut off from this mad world of ours.*

*This new job of ours is well underway. Of course, you understand that I can't throw much light on the subject for obvious reasons. My Lieutenant, Tolleson, and Steve, are out on the line ahead of the construction already. Each evening they return to the head of the clearing and sleep in wantegans (large house sleds that are equipped with bunks and a stove that are caterpillar drawn along the trail as construction progresses). Jim and I were left back here temporarily at a base camp to get together the rest of our equipment and arrange some details. In the meantime, we have been helping some officers  running a survey and spotting pole positions for a proposed telephone line along the new road. (Jim worked for a Michigan Power Co. doing transmission towers and pole survey work in civilian life). We are going to start the actual fieldwork to-morrow morning. I am going to "punch a gun"(operate a transit)and Jim is chief of the party.*

*This will be a rather interesting job, but I fear it will only last a few days for Jim and I. We were down to the radio shack this evening to see if any messages arrived for us. None had, but we saw one requesting that we be sent out ahead to work with "Arky", Steve, and the Lieutenant on a shift basis. I guess it's rugged country out there, and the snow is crotch deep on a tall Indian, so the boys are catching hell. Whatever happens, you can bet I'm going to be kept busy.*

*Tuesday Evening:*
*March 2, 1943*                    *Yukon Territory        Canada*

*Well, we are really way out in the bush again, almost 100 miles out from the base camps on the Alcan Highway. I rode out in a supply truck loaded with diesel fuel for the "cats" over the rough trail. The trip took us about 15 hours. Without a doubt that the roughest ride I ever had in my life. It's unbelievable the beating and abuse that modern mechanical equipment can take! It's a marvel that our truck wasn't beaten to a pulp by the time we arrived at the head of the clearing, but strange as it may seem, it was unloaded and started on it's, long, rough journey back, still going strong. Some of the pitch holes were so deep and rough, plus, being filled with a couple feet of water, that I got out and walked ahead, lest I get beaten up riding in the cab of the truck. Two trucks always travel together, so they can help each other through such rough spots. When I arrived here my back felt as if it was sun-burned from being chafed against the back of the seat as we continuously bounced along over the rough trail.*

*Our work out here is location again. It's pretty tough going because the snow up in this mountainous country is almost waist-deep on the level. This condition necessitates using snowshoes, when working out ahead of the lead "cat"! A good deal of the time, one of us rides the lead "cat" and guides the general location from the deck. That's a pretty rough go too. However, we change off so it's not too bad.*

*We are still fortunate, in that the weather continues to prevail. That* means a lot. The mountainous terrain we are passing through is quite beautiful. This is real wilderness up here. There are many large wolves which, due to the deep snow, are having a tough time of it here. There are caribou in this region too. Yesterday we ran across a fresh kill. The wolves had the poor caribou torn and chewed to bits. Only the hide and larger bones were left. Such an attack and kill must be a gruesome sight. "Nature in the raw is seldom mild."

We live in wantegans, a bunkhouse on a sled. These are drawn up ahead over the newly built trail each nite by the caterpillar. The cookhouse is mounted on a sled too. The food out here is good, but of course the hours are very irregular.

Our only contact with the outside is by radio. A radio car travels right along with the outfit. Sometimes contact cannot be made for a day or two, due to the electrical disturbances caused by the recent brilliant displays of the Aurora Borealis. The last few evenings they have been particularly active and beautiful. I wish you could witness them too.

Sunday Evening
March 10, 1943                                    Whitehorse, Yukon Territory


Not much is new up here to write about. Even though this mountain-ous terrain is plenty rugged and presents many location problems, we have been making quite rapid progress on this trail. Yesterday we advanced 11 miles. After supper they started towing our wantegons last night, and we didn't reach the end of day's construction until past midnight. Trying to sleep in your bunk as you rumble over rough trail is quite the stunt, but when you're tired enough, it's not impossible.

Every night I'm plenty tired from snowshoeing. This Tacon Indian with us is a demon on the webs. Another week at the most should get us into our destination. The Lieutenant and the other three boys have already left and have gone back to a road camp on the Alcan Highway. I'm staying out here to help see them through, and then I am to return to the camp where they are temporarily stationed. I dread the tough, long journey out to the Alcan over the tote road. It's a man-killer. I'm still in the dark as to what the future of we five holds. I don't know if our company is still on the West coast or not.

Golly, what scenery up in here! Sometimes I can scarcely believe my own eyes. The mountain peaks are so lofty that at times the summits are not visible due to snowstorms blowing up there almost at cloud level, yet down on the valley floor, the weather is calm, bright and pleasant. This is the Canadian sheep hunting country, of which we read such exciting tales in our Outdoor magazines. I've been watching the mountainsides, but have seen no big horns so far. The ice in these rivers is many feet thick and just as clear as glass. The water is pure and crystal clear. Some of the ice formations on the embankments are beautiful, frozen in rippling cascades.

*In this section the snow is not quite so deep, only knee deep.*

*I passed through a canyon this morning that was as rugged and picturesque as any I have ever seen. I'll bet that during the spring freshets that canyon is a raging torrent. The volcanic rock is as hard as flint and, due to the terrific pressure of weight of mountains and erosion of the swirling water, the canyon walls are twisted and gargled in grotesque shapes. The rock was in hues of all colors, some incredibly beautiful. That canyon would be a geologist's paradise.*

*A few days ago we came upon a deserted trapper's cabin. In it was an old rusted gold pan, probably a relic of the Yukon Gold Rush days. We ate our lunch in that cabin.*

*You are probably wondering how come I have time to write this letter. Due to lack of fuel we are temporarily held up, so we aren't moving tonight*

*Harry Spiegel*

Harry's final "letter home" from the Canol project.

## CANOL CREW SAYS FAREWELL TO THE NORTH

Lt. Lancaster and the four enlisted men left in Canada, arrived back in the states on March 24th 1943. Pending Limited Service Classification Lt. Lancaster was transferred out, and Lt. Throm was assigned as replacement. He with Sergeants Halfacre, Tolleson, and Spiegel and Cpl. Stephenson arrived in Australia in May 1943; completing the history of Company "A."

# CHAPTER XIV

# WRAPPING UP

## Extracts From Sid Navratil's Diaries

*January 2, 1943 Saturday*          *Camp McCoy, Wisconsin*

*There isn't much—as far as the camp is concerned—to complain about. We have spacious barracks and kitchen; the PX and Service Clubs just a few blocks away; dances every week, etc. However, we're back to GI routine that is distasteful to everyone.*

*January 4, 1943 Monday*

*Close order drills and snow shoveling, with a dash of Articles of War readings, were served to us today. The icy company streets made marching difficult as well as funny; but otherwise we found we all were still in pretty good form.*

*Furlough rumors are flying thick and fast again. The "reliable" source has it we're to have 10 to 15 days effective immediately, while another, just as reliable a one, claims the furlough is to be from 30 to 45 days, and is to come soon.*

*January 5, 1943 Tuesday*

*And so today we turned in our Arctic clothing, bedrolls and comforters. The bed roll was unspeakably dirty, not having seen the cleaner's for almost ten months. All the underwear has a dark gray tone, which only the laundry-man will fully appreciate.*

*January 11, 1943*          *Monday*

*These are our blackest days yet. Just when we were getting ready to go home on our 12 days' furloughs—half of the company is gone already—we were "alerted, which simply means that we are to leave for the Port of Embarkation very soon. The men out on furloughs are being recalled, and the rest of us are left with only a dark outlook. I don't expect to ever to see a more disconsolate bunch of men. We go through our tedious daily routine like automats, grumbling and swearing at the least provocation.*

*I had just sent letters home last night—telling them in the most exuberant terms to expect me home soon, and now I feel like a worm. However, there is still a chance—a good one—as our commanding officer, Capt. Stewart, is trying his darndest to get us what we so fully deserve. Mine, and everyone else's opinion in the Company of the Captain is of the highest esteem. He showed a great deal of consideration toward us since he took command. By giving the first half of the company their furloughs, he "stuck" his neck out, risking almost everything only for the benefit of his men. It isn't necessary to say that he has earned for himself the greatest devotion of men any officer could wish for. "And the Caissons go Rolling Along."*

*We will probably go to one of two places: Australia or North Africa. The outlook, therefore, would be a rather exciting one if, only if, we could go home even for a little while. God, to be so close to home and not being able to get there is driving me half crazy. Just like everyone else, I long to get away from these army faces and see the ones of my loved ones. This indeed is a very hard test to endure—as the strains of the "New World Symphony" fade away.*

*January 19, 1943*                 *Tuesday*

*There is feverish activity going on in the barracks. The clothing has been checked, teeth fixed, papers 'tended to'—and the furloughs made out! Our own cheerfulness is the height of gloom to the ones who just came back (about half of them married). Tomorrow morning, if nothing goes amiss, 1 leave this camp to forget the Army for ten short days.*

*A New Chapter is Beginning*

*February 1, 1943*            *Monday*            *Camp McCoy,    Wisconsin*

*And so begins the diary of a married man. While home on furlough it happened —just like that—and to say I'm glad would be putting it mildly. Now at last there is an aim; a reason why I should fight. And when the war is over she will again be there to help me face my—our— new life.*

Sid and Helen Narvratil - wedding day 1943.

HEADQUARTERS FORT ST. JOHN SECTION
ALCAN HIGHWAY
FORT ST. JOHN,  BRITISH COLUMBIA

21 December 1942

SUBJECT:     Commendable performance of duty.

TO:     The Officers and Men of Company "A," 648th Engineer Battalion
(Topographic)

1.  It was a cold wintry day last March when you arrived at
Dawson Creek for duty on the Alcan Highway.  Now, nine months
later, the highway is open, because you have completed your mission, you are leaving Dawson Creek, headed back to the States.

2.  You have played a leading part of the highway construction.
You have led the way in locating the toughest section of the road,
the stretch through the Canadian Rockies.  You have mapped the
southern half of the highway.  You have done all this and more,
too, under conditions as severe as those encountered by any group
of men, large or small, who participated in constructing the high
way.  Your performance of duty has been marked by intelligence,
industry, courage. Yours has been a hard job done well.

3.  We cannot let you leave without without telling you that we
have enjoyed serving with you.

R.D. INGALLS
Colonel, Corps of Engineers,
Commanding Officer

## UNIT CITATION

*The following is quoted from Section X, War Department General Order 16, dated at Washington, March 25, 1943.*

*"Citation of troop units engaged in construction of the Alcan Highway. The units listed below are cited for meritorious conduct in the construction of the Canadian-Alaskan Military Highway during the period March to October 1942:*
*18th Engineer Combat Regiment*
*35th Engineer Combat Regiment*
*93d Engineer General Service Regiment (cid)*
*95th Engineer General Service Regiment (cld)*
*97th Engineer General Service Regiment (cld)*
*340th Engineer General Service Regiment*
*341St Engineer General Service Regiment Co D*
*29th Engineer Topographic Battalion Co A*
*648th Engineer Topographic Battalion*
*73d Engineer Light Pontoon Company*
*74th Engineer Light Pontoon Company*
*The above units were charged with the task of constructing a 1,600 mile highway from Fort St. John. British Columbia, Canada, to Slana, Alaska, with all speed within the physical capacity of the troops.' The general route selected for the highway lay across vast areas of almost impenetrable wilderness, vaguely mapped and but little known. Commencing with the spring thaw and continuing through the summer floods, the troops overcame the difficulties imposed by mountain terrain, deep muskeg, torrential streams, heavy forests and an ever-lengthening supply line. By virtue of remarkable engineering ability, ingenious improvisation, and unsurpassed devotion to duty, the units assigned to the highway construction completed their mission in one working season, and thereby opened a supply road to Alaska that is of inestimable strategic value to the war effort of their country."*

## AWARD OF LEGION OF MERIT

"The War Department has advised that Tec. 4 Lester E. Tolleson, 39302563, 638th Engineer Topographic Battalion, has been awarded the Legion of Merit for service during the construction of the Alcan Highway, and that citation will be published in War Department General Orders"

It is brought to the attention of all concerned that the Legion of Merit is awarded to individuals who shall have distinguished themselves by exceptionally meritorious conduct in the performance of outstanding service. This is the fourth highest award a soldier can receive. The official announcement is received with great pleasure by this headquarters.

The above quoted from Daily Bulletin No. 248, dated Dec 1943, Headquarters, 648th Topo. Bn.

# Beyond the Alcan Highway...

Their surveying duties in British Columbia completed in 1942, "A" Company was deactivated, and the men were absorbed into other units of the 648th. Inspite of the argurous and grueling conditions encountered, no fatalities were suffered by the officers and men of the 648th Topo. Battalion.

At noon on the 26th of Febuary 1943 we took our last look at the Golden Gate Bridge and the shores of California; 25 days on the high seas lay ahead of us. The company furnished two officers and 155 enlisted men for security watch throughout the voyage which was without incident. On March 10th, exactly one year from the date we crossed the International boundry into Canada, we crossed the equator into the southern hemisphere. On the 23rd of March we debarked at Brisbane, Queensland, Australia.

The Battalion, known as the "Base Map Plant," was located in Melbourne, Australia, and had the task of mapping the Southwest Pacific.

"B" Company studied aerial photographs provided by Air Corps' P-38 and B-24 reconnaissance aircraft. The photos, after delineation, were made into maps, which were then sent to "C" Company for printing. Map depots were set up in Brisbane and in Hollandia, New Guinea. Headquarters Company had the responsibility of storing, transporting, feeding and otherwise caring for the Battalion.

Early in February 1945, orders were received to set up a new map plant in Manila. Australia had grown in the affections of the men stationed there, many of whom had married Australian women. A tearful "farewell" that followed will never be forgotten.

On April 7, 1945, the Battalion disembarked in Manila, a city lying in ruins. A sense of urgency to get the war over-with pervaded the unit, and within a relatively short time it was in operation once again. Just when it seemed to everyone that a costly invasion of Japan was imminent, in August 1945 news came of the bombing of Hiroshima and Nagasaki, and the war's end.

## Extracts From Sid Navratil's Diaries

*August 14 1945*          *Wednesday*          *Manila, Philippines*

*This is an entry that I have been long waiting to set down. The War is over, and the tired world is again quiet! Well, not quite so, as celebration is in full swing all over the states. For us GI's the question remains the same "When do we go home?"*

*December 13 1945*     *Thursday*

*This is the last entry is a four year diary. Today at aproximatle 2:15pm, I became a citizen-civillian. Now its "Good-bye" to the army!*

# Men of Company "A" 648th Topographical Battalion

| | | | |
|---|---|---|---|
| Adrian | Dittis | Kaplan | Ryan |
| J.L. Allen | Dotta | Kemp | Schlereth |
| N.E. Allen | Dunn | Klein | Schmitt |
| Alsup | Epstein | Knolkamper | Shafer |
| Andrews | Eschbach | Kassakowski | Smith |
| Aronica | Fariello | Krisovsky | Spain |
| Aurica | Finn | Krupa | Spiegel |
| Auringer | Fisher | Kumpe | Starkowicz |
| Bagel | Fontana | Kuppe | D. Stephenson |
| Bailey | Forziati | LaMonte | L. Stephenson |
| Baker | Foster | Lancaster | Stewart |
| Balog | Frank | Lawton | Sudholt |
| Baniszewski | Gamez | Lobaugh | Sullivan |
| Barnett | Gallucci | Lovin | Surratt |
| Basciano | J.P. Geradi | Ludwick | Syron |
| Baxevanis | R.S. Geradi | Marra | Taylor |
| Baysinger | Gleason | Mason | Teeter |
| Benavides | Goldschmidt | McClain | Throm |
| Birk | Goodman | McCormack | Tiddens |
| Bivens | Gras | Miduski | Tolleson |
| Blackmon | Graves | Montpetit | Tomlinson |
| Blair | Graziano | Myers | Trotter |
| Bollini | Gross | Navratil | Ulatowski |
| Borenstein | Gunning | Nelson | VanNice |
| Bourassa | Halfacre | Nesom | Villarreal |
| Bowden | Haliburton | Nowak | Vines |
| Branco | Halperin | O.Brien | Vuilleumier |
| Brennan | Hammonds | Olmedo | Walton |
| Bridson | Hart | Oullette | Warlikowski |
| Brown | Harwood | Peterson | Warren |
| Calci | Havins | Pierce | Webb |
| Caldwell | Hoffman | Police | Weidman |
| Campos | Hoppe | Price | Wetzel |
| Carr | Horan | Prochniak | Williams |
| Coccia | Huist | Reagan | Wilson |
| Coker | Hunt | Ridenour | Wood |
| Corbitt | Hurst | Roland | Wrigley |
| Cotter | Jackson | Ross | Wyhs |
| Cramblitt | Jenison | Rothenberg | Zaleski |
| Cunio | Jennerjahn | Russ | Zalewitz |
| Dameron | Jonhson | Russac | Zeisler |
| Daunhauer | Jordan | Rue | Zintak |
| Deem | Kalhorn | Ryan | |

# CHAPTER XV

# RECOLLECTIONS OF
# THE LOCAL PARTICIPANTS

The first-hand accounts, in words and photos of individual soldiers through their letters, diaries and recollections are be treasured as a unique insight into the remarkable feat of the Alaska Highway's construction. They do not however tell the full story, as the cast of characters also included local residents of the area, whose life would be forever changed by this wartime intrusion of thousands of men and heavy equipment carving out a road into their backyard.

A few of the local participants have had portions of the story from their perspective recorded ... most have not. With the passage of time, these recollections become forever lost. Stories of Archie Gairdner, described by some of the soldiers as a true "Iron Man" are riveting, but the story in his own words has not been recorded. He was highly respected by the local population, lived into his late eighties and has many descendants. Fort Nelson has a Gairdner subdivision, and Gairdner Creek in the Steamboat Mountain area, is named after him.

"Iron Man" Archie Gairdner - at his home in Fort Nelson - in the 1920's.
(Photo courtesy George Behn.)

*[Editor's note—This Clipping is from Edmonton Journal, 1942.]*

# 4 Brothers Lead Americans In Alaska Road Route Quest

## Will Take Men Into Uncharted Areas of Northwest
### TRAPPERS,     PIONEERS

By Don Menzies
(Edmonton Journal Staff Reporter)

DAWSON CREEK,   B.C.   , March 20.  When the saga of the Alaska highway is written four brothers, all trappers, traders and ranchers, will   figure prominently.

The brothers will take U.  S. engineer units by dog team into the uncharted areas between Fort St. John and Fort Nelson, and Fort Nelson and Watson Lake, to blaze the trail which eventually become the North American continents's most vital road.

They are Elisha, John, Dennis, and Lynch Callison, who operate a ranch north of Fort St. John and trading posts in the north including Fort Nelson.

These brothers have traveled over vast areas in the north by dog team and pack horseand have an excellent knowledge of Indian trails.  They even have blazed trails themselves.

The brothers will take American survey parties into areas which will be selected from reconaissance planes as logical routes for the highway.  The survey parties will study ground conditions, return and make their findings known, then start out to blaze the Alaska Highway.

*[Editor's Note—The following passage is taken from Heath Twichell's "Northwest Epic: The Building of the Alaska Highway," page (126-127). Used with permission of the author, Heath Twichell.]*

In late June, Col. Ingalls decided to send out two new ground reconnaissance parties. One, led by Eschbach, was to pick up the McCusker Trail beyond Steamboat Mountain and this time follow it all the way to Watson Lake. The other, led by Lieutenant Stewart, was to travel with Eschbach as far west as Muncho Lake and then split off and head north to confirm the feasibility of Curwen's alternate route to Watson Lake. Although the regiment had recently received a long-awaited set of low-altitude stereographic photographs covering both possibilities, these had been taken on a day when the high trail west of Muncho Lake was, as usual, covered by clouds. Before committing himself irrevocably to Curwen's route, Ingalls was determined to find out whether a better path lay beneath those clouds. A wrangler with a team of pack horses would soon be coming up from Fort St. John, Eschbach was told. These animals were for his use, now that they could find firm footing and plenty of forage along the trail. Eschbach could include as many of his own men in the party as he wished, Ingalls continued, but a native who knew every inch of the McCusker Trail had already agreed to be their guide. His name was Charlie MacDonald.

MacDonald lived in a small cabin midway along the McCusker Trail, in the high valley where MacDonald Creek joins the Toad River. A man of perhaps fifty summers, he trapped animals to support his wife, Nellie, eight or nine children (MacDonald was hazy about numbers), and his aged father, the patriarch of the family. It was not an easy, carefree life. That winter, when the dried fish and game ran out, Nellie had had to stretch their dwindling supplies of trading post canned goods with concoctions of boiled bark and herbs. MacDonald's bad teeth, short stature, and gaunt, deeply lined brown face told of enduring many such winters. His eyes, black and alert, also bespoke a persistent curiosity. Numbers may have flummoxed him, but maps did not—although, on the trail, MacDonald had no real need of maps. Eschbach would soon be glad of that.

Nellie MacDonald (in doorway) with her children.

The 35th Engineers first made Charlie MacDonald's acquaintance in mid-June, when he passed eastward through their forward base near the Kledo River on his way to Fort Nelson with a load of furs. Within a few days, his pack horses heavily laden with food and other supplies, he was back at the forward camp. In no apparent hurry to return home to his family, he hung around for several days, cadging free meals and quietly watching the goings-on. What fascinated him so much was not the noisy bulldozers; those he'd already grown used to at Fort Nelson. Rather, it was the white men's odd habits and endless hustle and bustle. Before long he was asking questions:

"What this?" and "Why you do that?" At first Ingalls thought this inquisitive native a pest, but eventually he recognized the quick intelligence behind his broken English. Moreover, the man claimed to know a pass through the mountains west of Muncho Lake where a road might be built. So Charlie MacDonald hired as Eschbach's guide.

One day, while Eschbach was still waiting for the pack horses from Fort St. John, MacDonald wandered into the regimental operations tent. There, Lieutenant Colonel Twichell was bent over a large table spread with dozens of aerial photographs, peering intently down at one pair of them through a binocular device mounted on short metal legs. Looking over Twichell's shoulder for several minutes, MacDonald finally asked, "Why you do that?"

Charlie Macdonald - late 1960's.
(Photo - courtesy of Wanda Sorell)

Nellie MacDonald - late 1960's.
(Photo - courtesy of Wanda Sorell)

Twichell tried his best to explain how the stereoscopic viewer worked, and that it made pictures of things seem real.  It helped him figure out the best pathway for the new road, he said.

"Me look?" asked MacDonald.

Twichell sorted through the photos, found the pair showing MacDonald Creek, adjusted everything, and let MacDonald take his place at the viewer.  There was no immediate reaction.  Then, as his eyes adjusted to the stereoscope, a three-dimensional image suddenly came into focus.  The startled native jumped about 3 feet.

"Me cabin!  Me cabin!" he shouted, pointing at the table top in surprise and delight.

Although Twichell obviously felt both affection and sympathy for Charlie MacDonald in recounting this tale, the white man's assumption of cultural and racial superiority is uncomfortably clear.  It would be interesting to hear MacDonald's  version of the same episode, but his is not recorded.

The MacDonald family's summer camp, Muncho Lake area, early 1970's.
Nellie and Charlie MacDonald in the rear.
(Photo - courtesy of Wanda Sorell, Charlie and Nellie MacDonald's granddaughter.)

Fort Nelson residents - 1942.
George Behn, Winnie Callison, Garnet
Harrold, Dennis Callison, Rita Parker.

*Following the unveiling of the Alaska
Highway Veterans and Builders monument
at the Fort Nelson Heritage Museum on
June 26th 2004, Garnet Harrold and
George Behn, were asked and agreed to be
interviewed. They served as wranglers
and scouts assisting the 648th topographical battalion during highway construction.
Award winning video producer Hank
Bridgeman, representing Hello North!
(Northern Rockies Alaska Highway
Tourism Association), Tourism Dawson
Creek and the Alaska Highway House,
recorded their stories, and permission to
use a portion of these interviews is greatly
appreciated and happily acknowledged
here.*

**Interview with Garnet Harrold: His story in his own words.**

I was 19 when I worked on the highway.

I remember when all the soldier guys suddenly showed up, most of the
native people, they didn't really... I don't know whether they were just afraid or
what, but I mean, lot of them were happy to see them. We met so many of them
and they were so nice to us. We really enjoyed it. I know, I had a lot of fun with
them on the highway when we were working with them. We used to sit down by
the campfire at night and then we tell jokes and stuff and they tell us jokes, and, you
know we'd have a great time. I enjoyed all the time I was with them. I really liked
it. They were a bunch of nice boys. Most of them I know were really nice boys,
very nice.

My job you see, I was packing the horses. There was a pack string that
came in from Fort St. John, was three packers, three guys. And then when they got
here, they pick up the other horses down from the Old Fort, some of them belonged
to Archie [Gairdner]. So, they got them horses too. I believe it was around 10 head
of horses that they got from the Old Fort.

And then later when Archie came home... Archie had to come home—his
wife  was having a baby or something. And they must have asked him who they
could get in the Old Fort. I knew Archie pretty good, because him and I, we used to
party on our same day birthday. We used to have quite a time. They brought
Archie home, they were coming down on the Jeep from Steamboat. And then they
came over and they saw me as Archie told them. And they asked me if I would go.

I said "Well, I'm not doing nothing." I said "Sure, I'll go with you."

So I got ready and they took me up to Steamboat Mountain, where the camp was. All the rest of the boys and the horse packers had already left that morning. They were going further up the road following the pack trail. They left me one saddle horse there. When I got there, the boys, they made me a lunch and they said "They left one horse for you so you can ride and you can catch up to them tonight." I knew the guy that owned the horses. I saddled up the horse and everything and I took off. They weren't too far ahead of me. They could only move so far every day, so I caught up early. From then on, well, I didn't see the cat train, because, where that store is at Steamboat right now, just above that, they went down below on a hill. They were working down there when we went by. So I never got to see the cat train. Well, actually, I did never see them until we were further up the highway. We were traveling, and I was gonna say that the cat train had pretty good going from after they left Steamboat because there wasn't much brush to cut. It's all open. So, I mean, they made good time. We were camped up along the Toad River there, later on. One of the officers came up to our camp and he says, he said "You boys had better be out of here in the morning early, because the cats are gonna be right on your tail. They're right back here. They're not very far." We got up at four o'clock in the morning and started wrangling horses. We we got them all packed and everything. We got them all tied off on a tree, and the cats were pushing dirt right there on the side hill. We had to get out of there because the horses were starting to get scared. So we started to untie them as fast as we could and we got them out of there.

That was in July.

We got away from the cats, and then we moved on every day. We got up to Muncho Lake. Then the cats came right behind us, not too far. It's all just clear sailing you know, down the Toad River there, there's no bush hardly at all, so they went right through to Muncho Lake. They caught up to us there. And we had to go over the mountain, with horses over the pack trail. There's three hills in there that we had to go over. We took the trail and started out to get away from the cats. But they were there for quite a little while, because they had that straight rock that came right out to the water and they had to do all that blasting, to get a road through there. That took a little... quite a while.

I had seen the cats before, at other times, in Alberta or somewhere. I'd seen no blasting or anything like that. We started over the mountain with the horses and we just got going down, starting down the second hill on the mountain, when smoke came up over the hill. A fire started at the cats, where the cats were working. Don't know how it started—but it started across the mountain. We got down, the horses could smell it right away, I told them, "We better get some going, we got to get out of here. That fire's coming our way." So we got down the third hill and then along the sandbar. We pushed them pretty hard through there just to get away from the smoke. When we got down to the other end of the lake and then we camped there with the horses. Some of the boys were down there, coming to talk to us. From then, we never got to see the cats anymore, because we left them there when they had to do all that blasting. We'd always root along in the bush... We always blazed a tree every so often and we marked the "R's" on there so that they knew it was ours. It was good traveling like that. I never did see the cats again. Actually, I don't think I'd seen the cat train again all the rest of that summer because once after we had left the Liard River, we had two parties survey crew with us. It's all right along the river all the way down right to the Liard pack trail. Once we crossed the Liard they got back up off the river bank and they had to start cutting the lines, the survey lines, for the cats. We didn't move very far. A lot of days, maybe we only moved about two miles. The officer says "Don't go too far, because" he says "we can't leave the boys cutting the trail." He says "We have to let them keep up to us very close. So we wouldn't move very far in a day. A lot of times, in the evening, we could hear them working, cutting the trail up on the hill, you know.

I never did hear anything about aerial photographs before them days. You know, I never did see any aerial photographs, nothing like that.

I remember we were across the Liard, the other side of the hot springs, and we were camped along the banks of the Liard there. We had the camp all set up at night and everything, and an officer was sitting there on one of the banks out on the river there and he was looking at a photograph, an aerial photograph.

He told me, "Garnet, when you move ahead about two miles or three, there's an island up there" and he said "where you see that island, that's where you will stop on the river, we'll wait there for the boys. When you stop and make camp," he said "you'll turn the horses out to feed." There wasn't too much feed for horses neither, in those days. "If you take them back in the point, at the bottom of the hill," he said "there's a long slough in there—grass. If you take them back in there, they'll have a good feed back there." So we did that. Then, I was curious, because, how did he know about a slough back there? I didn't know. So he was working and I was just sitting a ways from him, watching him. And he said "did you ever look in the aerial photographs, man?"

"No" I said "I've never even heard of them." I said "I've been curious about how you knew what was ahead of us." He said "You want to see them?" I said "Sure, I'd like to."

So he said "Come here, I'll show you." So he showed me the aerial photographs and I looked at it. You could see it so plain. Even on the banks of the Liard River and the other side, you could even see the spruce trees, you know. And he says "That's how we know." I was surprised. I had never known this was like that. I was wondering how they knew what was ahead of us. So I was pretty happy about that. We kept it going anyway. It was pretty good sailing.

Once we got across the Liard, then we couldn't go too far. We couldn't leave them, because we had two crews surveying—army boys—and we had to wait for them because they couldn't go too far in one day. They had to cut the line and mark and everything. I don't think we ever moved more than maybe two miles, at the most. One time an officer asked me, he said, "would you go back down along the river and when you hear the boys working up on the hill, tell them that I sent you up there to bring them back to camp."

So I went up there and I told them, "Lieutenant Stewart sent me up here, to get you boys, I have to take you back to the camp." He told me "Make sure they don't get away from you."

So I brought them down to the river bank and they can't miss the trail because there's a pack train there. Altogether we had 50 head of horses there, cause we had two survey crews and they had quite a bit of stuff to pack. I had a few saddle horses that we had some boys change off a ride once in a while. So I brought them down to the river bank, to the trail there and I started up the river towards our camp and most of them followed me.

Then one of the boys behind me hollered, "Garnet, some guys are going the other way."

I said "They can't go that way, that's where we come from." So I went back and told them "You boys can't go that way, we got to go up river here, it's not too far, if you go downstream, you're just gonna go back where we come from. You better follow me or else you might get yourself into a pile of trouble, because he told me not to let you guys get away from me."

They followed me then. We got to camp. I didn't say nothing because there was no problem anyway. I didn't want those boys to get into trouble just over that. We never had no problem with them at all, you know. If the officers told us that this was what we're supposed to tell them, they're supposed to do it.

When we left Muncho Lake, and we kept going with the horses and we got to the Liard. We had to make two rafts there because we had to raft all that stuff across the Liard, no boats or nothing there. Before we moved all that stuff across and the horses, the officer said "Maybe, a couple of you should take some pack horses and saddle horses and go back to Muncho where the cats are," he says "And get some grub before we cross the Liard, because, once we cross the Liard we won't see them for quite awhile."

So I went back and I think it was, if I'm not mistaken, one of the other boys, John came with me too and we went back and we picked up some grub from the cat train and we brought it back to the Liard and then we had to start getting ready to build these rafts so we could get all that stuff across.

You know, it was a good summer, because as long as I've ever known the Liard River—that part—I've never seen the water was that low.

There's a narrow place there. There's a sand bar on the other side, quite a long sand bar on the other side. So, I figured that's where the horses will come out and we'd be good there on the sand bar. So we rafted all that stuff across. Took us all day. We started about seven in the morning. Two rafts, and boy, then we'd have to pull the raft up the other side, far enough that we could make it back to this side to where the sand bar is, because, you know, with a raft you gotta make quite a distance because it is floating away. So we done all right there. We didn't have no problem.

The American boys, they had one raft and they watched. We made one for them. We showed them how to do it and everything. They done pretty good. The packers had the other raft, five of us. We got all that stuff across, then we'd swim the horses. We had to put the horses in there. Oh, they would get all excited, you know. Archie Gairdner's buckskin had a colt on the road. It wasn't too big when we got to the Liard. But he could swim though.

If I'm not mistaken, I think we had around 50 or 51 head of horses—and one mule. The boys had brought that mule from Fort St. John. They said when they got to Fort Nelson, that one mule got away from the other one somewhere. They never did find it. And we were gonna push the horses in the water and I told them, "What we're gonna do. I'm gonna put Archie Gairdner's horses from the Old Fort up in the front." I says "I know that they'll take to water good, and when they do the other ones will probably follow." And so we did it.

They said "You're gonna let that little colt swim?"

I said "Yeah, he's gotta swim. He'll like it" They wanted to put him on the raft. I said "No, we don't." So we pushed them, and they all took to the water pretty good once the others started. The little colt as soon as his mother got in, he went right in with them. Smart. Stayed on the lower side of his mother, away from the current. They got a little over halfway across, it wasn't really that wide there, about half way in the middle. I said "You watch now, that colt is right beside his mother." The colt just went up and he threw up his leg over his mother's back and he rode her. Yeah, they couldn't believe that.

They said "How would a horse know to do that?"

I said "Well, you know, that's their ways. I guess they know." He even just hung onto his mother until he hit bottom and he got out and he walked out. They couldn't believe that. I never thought a horse, a colt would know that much. So we got across. We camped there on the other side, because we were working all day and we were tired too. We just let the horses go up on the hill and feed around. We made a camp there right on top of the bank.

One funny thing, the boys had the kitchen crew, they done all the kitchen work. They were a pretty good bunch of boys. We were camped once along the river and after we had everything settled down and we had supper then they were gonna put on a little show for the boys. Nothing to do, they were gonna play cowboys and Indians. They started putting on this show. This one guy, I didn't realize, had a knife on the side. They started wrestling, you know, like the movies. They had this guy down and he pulled that knife and he... just missed that guy right beside him. An officer jumped up. He thought he got him.

"No more of this. That was too close. You should never... you should never have knife like that." He says "If you wanna play later, you can put on a show or what you wanna do, but" he says "no knives or nothing." It was better after that, but I don't think the kitchen guy, really meant anything, he was just trying to play.

They paid us five dollars a day. But not the American Army. There was a Canadian guy by the name of was Burt Sheffield. He had the contract for these horses. The army would pay him and he'd pay us. That's the way it worked. So, when the job ended and we come back, I got back to the Old Fort on October 30th, I think, with Archie's horses, and the other boys. I don't know if they trucked the horses from here or they walked them. I couldn't say for sure. We had to go to Fort St. John to get our money. They said "You'll go there and you'll get paid there." So, we flew down to Fort St. John. It wasn't right away, it was a few days later, when we went down there. The guy that was supposed to pay us, he was there all right, but the officers and staff that I was looking for had already went back to the States.

When I found out that we didn't get paid our full amount of pay, I told them, "How come? We got more money than this coming. I've been working three months for this outfit. It seems like I only got maybe half my pay or a little better. That's all." And we couldn't do anything because there was nobody there now to back us up, eh. They had already had left. So that kind of hurt us a while. Oh the heck with it, I can't do nothing because, you know, they had already gone back. Sheffield got paid but, you know, he was just too crooked. And I often wondered. I meant to ask Archie if he had got paid for his horses because his horses was supposed to be getting two dollars a day for each horse. I never did ask him so I don't know if Sheffield beat everybody. I know that I never got my money.

*****

**Interview with George Behn: His story in his own words.**

I'm 80 now. Back in those days, I was 16 and 17 down at the Old Fort, the original Fort Nelson.

You noticed on that monument that was just unveiled, those three fellows, three soldiers standing beside my dog team, they were the first three that arrived down at the Old Fort. But they had their camp where the quarter master camped near here. I was at the Old Fort all my life, born and raised there. I was living with Mr. and Mrs. George, the white people, okay. They had a boarding house and a store, general store, you know. They're Americans too. They'd been in Canada many years, prior to this and all the excitement that went on. For us people, native people, it's something out of this world when you see all the Americans, the soldiers, the young men, all the equipment.

It was something new to us, you know. The people used to drive dog teams... that was all the transportation back them days. We'd drive up from the Old Fort, which is about by dog team trail, maybe about 15 miles. We used to watch the cats working, you know. All these guys setting up. And oh, it is just like watching TV today. It was really interesting.

In the summertime, some people used pack dogs. We used them all year round, eh. And horses, very few horses. It was getting more all the time. When the highway went through, a lot of the horses, from the South. You probably seen them on the pictures, you know. Just lots of them.

When, I started out, I was borrowed. As a guide... borrowed from Mr. and Mrs. George, you know, for a few days. And this guy, he didn't even know how to pack a horse. I didn't realize that. But I knew. I knew how and I went with him. We went to Fort Nelson and we camped at Mile 40, just past Kledo. It was 11 o'clock at night when we stopped. And four o'clock in the morning, we're on the road again, you know. We caught up to the reconnaissance crew. The main guide was Charlie MacDonald.

He's from up there. He lives up there year round, eh. And he had that section. Archie Gairdner, from the Old Fort, had the other one, and I filled in little party here and there. I was with the marking the centre line crew.

I used to work with them in my spare time, okay. When we're not using the horses, I just checked them in the morning and I'd go with them during the day when hauling supplies or whatever, eh. The communication was bad and the transportation was bad, because a flood was on at that time too. The main camp, the 35th Engineers, were at Kledo Creek. They were crossing on the pontoon bridge. And the next two, three miles, in the flood plain, the Muskwa, that was flooded too.

I go as far as I can, and from there... One spot I waited two days, you know, for supplies to come from the quarter master down here in town. Two days I waited. And finally one small cat came through. I believe it was a D4, you know, crawling around in the bushes. And I've seen three big ones, D8s, stuck right in the mud, you know, right over the track, the mud. And I think that guy, Chester, is here, he's one of these cats. So when I got back, about one in the morning, maybe a little later, with the supplies what they brought, and they had those big loafs of bread. I don't know how many of those, we had. Four of those guys, as soon as I come in, even that early, you know, and they just tied right into it. We were eating hot cakes three times a day.

With me, because I'm brought up here in this country, I knew how to rough it, and even for me it was pretty hard. But these young fellows, those soldiers you know, maybe some of them had experience... but I had a feeling that they just came out of the cities. They went through a lot. But, no complaint—nothing. They just did their best. I felt pretty bad about it at times, you know.

We got along with them really well. Even as young as I was, they listened to what I had to say. Like, for instance, one time, one of the corporals, and one of the other guys. They came in and they said "Well, we have to go back." So they asked me to go with them. And I did on foot... I went with them. They had spent three days in there before, prior to that. But I went with them and took some shortcuts, you know, so we got the information that they wanted, in a day. I knew that country... well, born and raised... like a squirrel or whatever, you know. I knew every bit of it. I'm used to the bush anyway.

These boys that I was with, the 648th, Reconnaissance Group, they're pretty well dressed well, for back in them days. Not like today, you know, insulated everything. Just the common good stuff, you know. Of course, in the winter time, we wore moccasins and they wore leather boots, you know. They got along well.

As far as the pay, well, the contractor gets the money. And I believe I got five dollars a day. Well, with the Indian people, we had no value of money at all. Today, if I had hung on to the money that I made, I'd be a rich old man but I got nothing. In one hand and out of this one, you know. It's always been like that. The value of money, you know, it's... People never complained about the wages, or whatever, eh. Even the oil exploration days, you know, 1947, 48, and 49, I got five dollars a day from Phillips Petroleum, and work all the hours you want, but the pay doesn't move at all.

I really enjoyed it, being with those soldiers, you know, and... really enjoyed it. I kinda overstayed my time, I kinda felt pretty bad when I left them, eh. And, this other fellow here, Garnet Harrold that you met, he replaced me. So I went back to my old job. With guardians, you know, Mr. and Mrs. George.

They done a lot for me. What little experience I got, in the white man's world, I got some experience, good experience from them. Like schooling. I never went to school because there was no facility. But I worked with the girls that worked for them, you know, after hours. It all depends how tired they were. I used to study with them at night, eh. Even after I was married, I used to go to the teacher and get some school book for a week. I used to study by the campfire, in the winter time. So, that's where I learned to read and write a bit.

Some funny things happened when this was all going on. The camp was at 335 Kledo Creek, the main camp was on our west bank, on the Fort Nelson side. And we were down on a flat on the opposite side of the river. They were putting in pontoon bridges and so on, you know. And there was a heck of a commotion going on at the camp up there so I had to go over there and see. They had a bear up a tree right in the centre of the camp. One guy was gonna push it down, get a cat to push it down. And the officer stopped him, said "No let him come down on his own." And that bear don't stay up a tree very long, that bear had to come down. You take lots of men there. When that bear hit the ground, and it took off, it didn't give a damn, if people were standing in the way. People just falling over the place, you know, and that bear took off. That's the funniest thing we seen.

The worst thing that happened, doing the job, I was coming in with horses to pick up supplies. The river was high. Steamboat Creek was, you know, bank to bank. There's no other way getting across. So, being young, I just rode my saddle horse in and the two pack horses behind me. Where the road came in the other side, well, the current took us down and we went down three bends on the creek before we come ashore. It really, give a person a funny feeling, you know. I was feeling like bailing off the horse, eh. But I thought I better not, because, you know, the horse, there'd be no controlling it.

You know, they'd been out there for two, three weeks, there, and the transportation was bad. Getting the stuff from here, a certain point, but there was a gap you can't get across and so on. Like I said, we ate hot cakes three times a day. But we did get some C rations. And those boys, they didn't seem to complain about that. But to me it was, that was a meal. We had hash, sandwich spread or whatever, and biscuits... harder than heck, but edible. And some hard candy in there, and I think there was five cigarettes, and a package of juice that you could mix. It was quite all right. And we caught some rabbits. I'm used to snaring rabbits anyway, otherwise you would never survive. I used to set snares in the evening, and go through it in the morning and we had maybe half a dozen rabbits. And, I'll clean 'm and roast 'm to the campfire.

They had surveyors, running a plane-table. You could see this station to station. But when you get in the bush, like out here, you went by the sound. You know, they have, the line cut here to there to here, and maybe you're four or five hundred feet over there, and you went by the sound and you shout, eh. And they take a bearing and you mark that place and you blaze a trail to this point, and cut that line out, and then the surveyor takes his sites and he move up and just on and on.

We had some ribbon, but mostly trail blazing, because not too many people back in those days had ribbon. We had a bit of red cloth and stuff, but we blazed the trees. I remember one point, we went this way, around, just about—even with the camp. The camp, I would say, oh heck, maybe half a mile, over here is where we started before, see. We were going this way, making a big loop here. I told Sergeant Gras, "You know, we just go right across here. Our camp is just across the little valley there." "No," he said, "we better stay on our trail."

But I said "No, you look at it." So I climbed a tree, and I could see the smoke. So I said "You come up here and look at it."

So he looked at it and he said "by golly, you're right." So, I led them through to the camp. It only took us about 20 minutes or so, maybe half an hour, and we were home.

And after that, you know, they followed me. They figured I was a pretty good navigator, because I lived in the bush all my life. I had to leave them, I kinda felt pretty bad. I went to Steamboat Mountain with them. When I came back I had three crippled horses. So I led those horses back. I made it from 335 to Airport in one day. And, it was a long day for me, I mean, for anybody, you know, walking. [over 40 miles]

As a kid I remember in the spring time the scouts, brought supplies, down the Sikanni River, Old Fort, and on down, eh. There was four or five freighters the scouts lined up there along the shore. My grandmother had a night line for fish, so me and my cousin, we went down there, and we got a couple of fish. We come up the little trail onto the path that the people travel, and we said, well maybe somebody will come and take the fish away from us. Then we got on the trail and here's this guy coming and he was talking away, you know, and... I don't know what he was saying, but I remember to this day, just like he said it this morning: "Just a minute." I remember that word well. But we didn't know what it meant. We just took off in the bush, and hid our fish and went home. So that's that. That was Lynch Callison. A well-known family, those guys. I guess most of them passed on. At the moment, I understand it's only one man left out of that family. Yeah, they... Good trappers, good hunters, you know. I worked for them for many years. I had lots of experience from them,. Tough as a nail. I remember, one guy, I used to work for him, and we get up for breakfast at six o'clock, okay. Some guy is still staggering around. He'll come in and say "Hey, it's six oclock. You're still sleeping. How do you expect to get a day's work in," you know.

I enjoyed life well. I done what I wanted to do. With little experience, but I had ambition, and I watched the other people do things, you know. And I wanted to do the same thing. Even things that I never seen done or I watched the other people talk about it, and I just could picture it and I think about it. When it come down doing it, you know, I just about know how. It came naturally. And I traveled with different people, lots of people. That's where my experience come from. And I don't regret anything at all, you know.

# CHAPTER XVI

# VETERAN'S MONUMENT BECOMES A REALITY

After the war ended, men of the 648th Topographical Battalion, like former soldiers everywhere, reverted back to civilian life. These men took a great deal of pride in the claim that they helped survey and build the Alcan (Alaska) Highway.

Harry and his brother, Carl, did eventually travel the highway some 40 years later. "Lots of fishing and photography, no clock to punch, truly some of the most carefree years of our lives."

Sid Navratil, who before the war had graduated from the Carneige school of art and design, (and had drawn the cartoons that appear in Alcan Trail Blazers), returned to his passion for the arts and succesfully operated a studio, and raised a family with Helen, back home in Pittsburg.

Sgt. Chris Gras returned to raise his family and run a store in his home town of Rock Springs, Wyoming.

On the Alaska Highway in Fort Nelson, a museum opened up in the 1980's to preserve the local history, including its Alaska Highway heritage.

At the well attended May 2003 Fort Nelson Historical Society regular monthly meeting, passages of the just received Harry Spiegel letters were read aloud. Never before in the 25 year history of the society was a presentation met with a standing ovation. "Harry's letters home" were that good. A suggestion was made to honour, with a memorial, the two outfits shipped to Fort Nelson, the 35th Company Combat Engineers and the 648th Topographical Battalion. These were "our boys," working in "our backyard." This received unanimous approval.

More delightful encounters with our Alaska Highway history makers occurred throughout the year. Helen Navratil sent along the diary Syd had kept all through his Alcan experience—another thoughtful observer of history in our back-yard. Pictures too ... about 200 of them.

She attended the 648th reunion group meeting in Milwaukee and kept them abreast of our plans. She sent off letters to all the surviving members of "A" Company, encouraging their wholehearted support for the efforts of the Fort Nelson Heritage Museum. Helen Navratil is one heck of a gal!

Remember Sgt. Chris Gras's daughter Karen in Colorado? She located some of that old home movie that her dad had taken. It had been shot in colour! It was professionally transfered to DVD, and not only that but George Behn, one of the scouts mentioned earlier, could identify many of the men and locations. Much of what Harry had written home about came to life in the rare, ten minute, 60 year old footage. If not for the suggestion of Harry and Carl Spiegel, this never would have come to light.

A few other fine folks have given generously of their time and expertise … including retired, award winning historian Col. Heath Twichell. His book, "Northwest Epic—the building of the Alaska Highway" is probably the best written account on the subject. He has helped with US Army Dept. of History contacts, and has been a great source to confirm facts and consult for ideas. His father was Col. Heath Twichell, who for some time commanded the 35th Company Engineers, and was in Fort Nelson Easter Sunday 1942, as was Chester Russell and the 648th Topographical troops.

Another commanding officer attached to the 35th Engineers was Col. James McCarty. He was on hand at Contact Creek Sept 15, 1942, along with Chester Russell and the 648th Topographical troops. Although McCarty passed away in the 1970's, his son Edward McCarty stopped by for a visit a couple years ago. "Keep me in mind if anything is ever done to recognize these troops for their contribution," said Edward. The McCarty family was pleased to make a contribution to the monument construction costs.

And then … while listening to a piece on the CBC radio program "As It Happens" on Remembrance Day, they had as a guest the fellow who designed the memorial for Canadian troops killed in Afghanistan. It took me over a week to track the fellow down (Rod McLeod, he lives in Calgary), but I found and e-mailed him to let him know what we were up to, and could I find out more details from him about what he does, what he'd need from us, what he costs, etc.

His reply, about six hours later, was "I would be delighted to work with you on this project, as my father was heavy-duty mechanic on the Alaska Highway construction." Then, when I saw an example of his memorial, the hair on the back of my neck stood up again. Using a combination of the unit's crest, photos and maps combined with industry leading laser engraving… Wow! Our monument designer was on the team.

And so, a major event was planned for June 26th, 2004 in Fort Nelson—the creation and official unveiling of a monument at the Fort Nelson Heritage Museum, dedicated to the highway's wartime construction contribution of both the 648th Topographical Battalion, (the Alcan Trail Blazers), and of the 35th Company Combat Engineers. Both of these outfits were shipped straight to Fort Nelson before spring breakup in March 1942 to build the highway. These were "our boys" working in "our backyard."

Hmmm… remember the unanimous approval to create a monument to honour the 35th Combat Engineers and 648th Topographical battalion? These things don't happen all by themselves. In fact, much scratching of the ol' noggin has taken place to consider something unique, tasteful and appropriate. Dear ol' dad suggested utilizing some Cat parts for the 35th Engineers; the watchful eye will see cat sprockets and parts incorporated into the monument stonework. The "Survey" silhouette atop the monument was carefully crafted by Marl Brown—to represent the image of "Sgt. Jennerjahn at the transit"—(Photo in the Feb '43 issue of "National Geographic").

\*\*\*\*\*

**Northern Rockies Regional District**

Town Square, 5319-50th Ave. S. Bag Service 399,
Fort Nelson, BC, Canada V0C 1R0
Tel (250) 774-2541  Fax (250) 774-6794
www.northernrockies.org

## Recognition Day of Building the Alaska Highway
### June 26th, 2004

**WHEREAS** honouring the hard work and dedication made by the 12,000 troops and 7,500 civilians who constructed the Alaska Highway and acknowledging the incredible sacrifices and hardships faced by all the workers is important; and

**WHEREAS** we specifically recognize those troops working out of the Fort Nelson area, Co. "A" 648th Topographical Battalion and 35th Combat Engineers, U.S. Army and those residents whose local expertise was integral to completion of their mission; and

**WHEREAS** it is meaningful to recognize that the building of the Alaska Highway project began in 1942 with the setting down of 8 miles of road a day, 7 days a week, using 11,500 pieces of equipment for 1,522 miles and completing it only 8 months later; and

**WHEREAS** we are thankful to the joint efforts of the Canadian and United States Governments for realizing the great Alaska Highway is a major transportation and communication link for all Northern communities, starting in Dawson Creek, BC and ending in Fairbanks Alaska.

**THEREFORE**, It is with great pride that I hereby proclaim June 26th, 2004 as a recognition day for all those dedicated individuals who helped build the Alaska Highway.

**Mayor Chris Morey**

# The Fort Nelson News

*June 30, 2004.*                            *Judith Kenyon, Editor*

## The Alcan Builders Receive Their Due as the Monument is Dedicated to their Efforts

The veterans and builders of the Alaska Highway were honoured on Saturday at an official ceremony where a plaque and memorial was unveiled.

"The Alaska Highway is an oddity, in that usually war breeds destruction, this Highway was an act of creation. It would profoundly change the north, connecting people and creating opportunities for so many," the Reverend Sandy Ferguson said at the dedication and unveiling of the monument recognizing the Veterans and Builders of the Alaska Highway.

Chester Russell, Henry Geyer, George Behn and Garnet Harrold were recognized for their work on the project.

Family members of the men who worked on the project came to Fort Nelson for the opening ceremonies carried out on Saturday in the beautiful sunshine in front of the museum.

RCMP Staff Sergeant Tom Roy resplendent in his scarlet, Mayor Chris

Part of the crowd on hand for the unveiling (Sgt. Gras' descendants on right).

Morey, and Director Shelley Middleton welcomed the guests. Ms. Sue Hay's students sang 'O Canada'followed by the 'Star Spangled Banner.' The flags of the two nations were unfurled.

Earl Brown, who spearheaded the whole enterprise, welcomed guests noting that the original idea was to create a monument recognizing the 648th Topographical Battalion, the 35th combat engineers, and the local trappers who worked on the road from Fort Nelson north. When the Alcan Trailblazers was published in 1992, it was hoped to raise enough money from the sales of the book to create a monument. Although plans fell short, a $480 (US) cheque went towards the project, augmented by donations from the museum society and Fort Nelson Rotary club, who president Val Lefebvre thanked those who had made the beautiful highway and town possible by their work.

Families of the soldiers who worked on the project were introduced including the family of Sergeant Gras, his daughters Karen (and husband Pete) and Diane, grandchildren Wade (wife Cyndi), Lisa, and Laura, great grand children Joshua, Devon, and Kelsey.

Henry Geyer, making his second recent visit here said when he first came he hated the place "it was  -30 to -40 below for months." Last year he returned by plane and when he landed he said "I realized it was all worth it, it's beautiful!"

Chester Russell brought his family family "to show them what it was all about." He has written a book about his time on the highway which was dramatized into a play. Chester got the idea when a friend sent him a picture of the Liard River bridge and he contacted Earl Brown, whose name was on the back of the postcard, saying he had photographs of the construction he might like to share.

Helen Navratil - was there with her family. She was one of the people involved who originally produced the Alcan Trailblazers book.

Her children Jeneen, Judith and Jon were there to recognize the work of their father Sid.

George Behn worked as a wrangler and a navigator on the Simpson Trail. "I really enjoyed seeing the new faces and some of the people who I knew and worked with. I remember being a little Indian out in the bush and suddenly there were cats and equipment, thousands of men...all working together."

Garnet Harrold who worked on the route along with another wrangler and guide Archie Gairdner, was there with his family and members of the Gairdner family. Archie was described as "nothing less than an Iron Man" by one of the soldiers recounting his work on the trail.

Messages came from the family of Col. James McCarty who thanked those who had engineered the monument for their thoughtfulness and hard work.

Harry and Carl Spiegel said it would be appropriate to honour "the local trappers, as they served as guides, the 35th Combat Engineers and the 648 Topographical Engineers, that collectively built the Alcan Highway in 1942."

The family of Sgt. Earl Fisher sent greetings from Dallas.

Heath Twichell, on behalf of his father, the late Heath Twichell Sr. said: "The work was done under the toughest conditions imaginable. during the tense and difficult time after the attack on Pearl Harbour, and an enduring bond has been forged between US and Canada - friends along the highway over the 62 years... My father, Col. Heath Twichell, who was one of the key leaders of the project, is remembered. If he was alive he would be flattered but he would be quick to remind you that it was not the leaders but the thousands of men who worked on the highway that made it possible."

Kris Valencia, Milepost editor, wrote "We salute you who help us remember them."

Carol Urquart-Fisher, a daughter of one of the soldiers telephoned good wishes from Adelaide, Australia the night before the dedication.

Rod McLeod, monument artist, from Calgary designed the project, and was delighted and honoured to participate, as his father Alex McLeod had been a heavy duty mechanic who worked on the highway's wartime construction.

United Church Minister Sandy Ferguson said "It is a tribute all the people who took part in its building, a celebration of their labour and commitment and a reminder of the price that had to be paid to build this Highway. Hopefully it will be a reminder for generations to come of what an awesome accomplishment this Highway is.

One of the most profound achievements of this Highway is that it is a potent reminder of what can be done when people come together in a common cause. This road was hacked out of wilderness in the face of so many obstacles.

Yet they, knowing of the importance of their work, continued to labour. In the midst of war, they were creating something that would change people's loves forever.

Today many people drive along the Highway and are able to witness the joys of creation in all it's majesty, thanks to the labour of those who came before them. When I first arrived here I discovered a poem about this highway which says the writer was unsure that whoever designed this Highway was 'driving in, or out of Hell!'

Although it's fair to say that this road is fairly difficult to drive, I prefer to see this Highway as a glimpse not of Hell, but of Heaven, because it's a powerful symbol of the good created when people are united in a common cause. So let us gather our thoughts and prayers and give thanks to all the people who laboured in the building of this Highway.

We aks for God's blessings on this memorial so that it was be a reminder of humanity's ability to create good out of the darkness of war. May this memorial continue to be an inspiration to follow in the footsteps in the footsteps of those who went before us, struggling to build a better world in which we will fulfill the blessings of God's creation."

Others involved in the project included Historical Society President Ray Nairon, Curator Marl Brown, The Executive Members, Staff and Volunteers of the Fort Nelson Historical Society.

Hand Routered Veterans and Builders sign: Darren Rice. Monument Construction & Stonework by Greystone Concrete & Masonry: Shane Anderson, Allan Smith, Peter Rideout, Lorrie Leslie. Surveyors Sihloutte: Marl Brown. Monument Designer: Rod McLeod. Produced by: LASER Etch Technologies Calgary

Afterwards a pot luck supper organized by society president Ray Nairon, members and volunteers, was held at the Trapper's cabin and garden attended by more than 300 people.

*****

*[Editor's note—Thanks to "The Fort Nelson News" for allowing reprint of this article and photographs.]*

The Road Builders who unveiled the monument to recognize the men who worked on the Alcan Highway. Left to right Henry Geyer, Garnet Harrold, Rose Harrold, Maggie Gairdner, George Behn, Chester Russel.

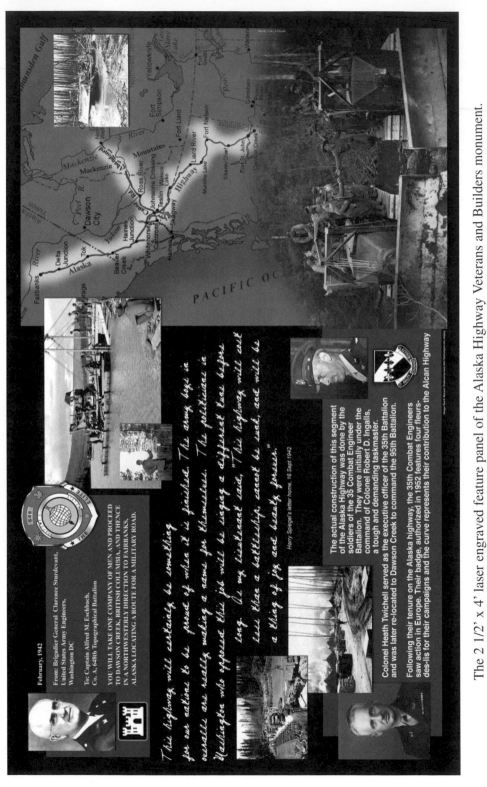

The 2 1/2' x 4' laser engraved feature panel of the Alaska Highway Veterans and Builders monument.

## "FORGOTTEN HEROS" FAMILY'S REFLECTIONS

I am unable to find words that are sufficiently adequate to explore my feelings of gratitude to you, your parents, the members of the Ft. Nelson Historical Society; all those involved in the design, execution and dedication of the Ft. Nelson Monument "to the unknown heroes of 1942," those who found and built the original Alaska

The Navratil family - Helen, Jeneen, Judy, and Jon view the nearly completed monument.

Highway's southern end. The location of the monument is ideal, standing proudly in front of the Fort Nelson Heritage Museum, easily seen from the Alaska Highway.

The Monument is everything those "forgotten" heroes could wish for—an acknowledgement that their efforts opened the way to the magnificent Highway their road has become. Thank you all!

The children and I enjoyed our visit to northwestern Canada. It was a long and somewhat wearing drive from Dawson Creek to Liard Springs. It was daunting to see the Highway stretching on and on—"miles and miles of miles and miles." I kept thinking of Sid trudging these weary miles on foot and recording those steps.

We especially thank you again, and all those involved in the realization of my dream; the Memorial to all those involved in the finding and building of the southern section of the Alaska Highway. Thank you, thank you!

Much love, Helen Navratil

It is difficult to put into words what an emotional event it was for me and my family to attend the unveiling of the monument in Fort Nelson. Standing in the places that my dad, Chris B. Gras, stood and realizing what a truly monumental job those men had accomplished in less than a year in 1942, gave me a tremendous sense of pride. Dad talked about that job his whole life, but he was not a bragging sort of person, so none of us ever appreciated what a difficult and marvelous thing he and all the men had done. My only regret is that he didn't live long enough to attend the unveiling and see what a great road it has developed into. He would have been in his glory to be able to visit with the men that worked with him like George Behn, Garnet Harrold, Chester Russell...

Thank you Earl Brown and all of Fort Nelson for making it all possible.

Karen Cecchinelli

On behalf of my husband, Col. James A. McCarty, and our children, I would like to thank the people of Ft. Nelson for keeping alive the memory of the 35th and 648th divisions of the US Army Corps of Engineers. When my husband reached out to shake hands at Contact Creek, he knew the effort to get through the cold, dangerous winter and hot, buggy summer had been worth it ....although, while reading his letters I wasn't always sure. In later years, he always spoke proudly of the memories of the ALCAN Highway and of his hope to revisit.

Because he did not, and to honor his memory, my children and I retraced his steps from Ft. Nelson to Contact Creek a few years ago and shared a great deal of the emotion and pride he must have felt. Thank you for making this memorial possible.

Elizabeth McCarty, widow of Col. James A. McCarty, 35th Engineers, and the McCarty family.


It has been most interesting working with Earl L. Brown of Fort Nelson, British Columbia, both with preparing to publish an updated version of "Alcan Trail Blazers" and of course with the monument construction honoring the members of Company "A" of the 648th.

We would have loved to be at Fort Nelson for the dedication, but it's an impossible dream due to frail health, and age that will see Harry turn 90 at his next birthday. You can bet that we were proudly there with you in spirit.

It has been a great and uplifting experience for Harry and me being involved, in a limited way, with the Fort Nelson Historical Society and Earl Brown this past year, and knowing that the men who made up the Alcan Trail Blazers, true heros, are forgotten no more.

The "Spiegel boys" in Buffalo - Harry & Carl

Monument unveiling day - Fort Nelson Heritage Museum.
George Behn, Garnet Harrold, Chester Russell, Henry Geyer.

# CHAPTER XVII

# SO WHO THE HECK IS
# EARL L. BROWN?

The Alaska Highway has been my home since 1957, and over the years I've developed a passion for its history. Raised at the Army Highway Maintenance camp at Mile 245, and then across the road at our family's highway lodge for many years before moving to Fort Nelson, I've enjoyed the opportunity to meet many of the highway's old-timers, and folks who were involved in its original construction.

After high school, I went directly into public accounting, and continue to this day. Life is too short to be parked behind a desk as a number-wrestler full time, and I have developed other interests, taking leave of absence from accounting several months each year. These other interests include photography, an interest in the Bartlett Scenic Postcard business, and since 1985 I've also worked on assignment as Field Editor for The Milepost travelbook. As well as postcards, I've published two full colour photo view books, one on the Northwest Territories, and one on the Alaska Highway.

In 1992 I took a workshop with self-publishing authority Dan Poynter in Santa Barbara, California. In 1997 I returned to California for another workshop with Mark Victor Hansen and Jack Canfield, the co-authors of the "Chicken Soup for the Soul" series of books. Dan Poynter and other experts in the field were part of the presentation team... Wow, what a learning session!

Over the years as a member of the local historical society, Toastmasters International, and Rotary, my Alaska Highway heritage interest has grown. I was happy to assist Arthur Black and his producers on their 2000 "Basic Black: Alaska Highway show." Later, I felt there was a need for a quality video of the Fort Nelson area, and produced "So... you want to know more about Fort Nelson... eh?" Recently, Chester Russell's self published "Tales of a Catskinner" book was going to be out of print. At 82, Chester had run out of steam as well as books. The story was way too good to let die, so we agreed that I'd republish the book, and now Chester enjoys receiving royalties.

Several of my projects have been done "on a shoestring," or done because it was "the right thing to do" ...and worry about the dollars later. In each case, quality of the project was important. (Of course with the influence of my folks,

Marl and Mavis Brown, this is understandable. It's said that you should choose your parents carefully... a heck of a good job in this case.) I feel strongly that the completely revised "Alcan Trail Blazers" is an important part of the Alaska Highway heritage, and had to be done to the best of my ability.

It's mind boggling to realize that I've spent far more time reviewing, fact checking, and polishing the material for this book that it took the Alcan Trail Blazers to build the original highway in the first place! But what an opportunity, to make contact and become fast friends with some of these Alcan Veterans and their families. What a thrill to bring to life these first hand accounts from such a splendid cast of characters.

Future projects include serving as the incoming president of the Fort Nelson Rotary Club for 2005/2006. Another is to be involved planning and carrying out a challenge for the community to enter the Guinness Book of World Records, for the largest water balloon fight in history—on June 18th, 2005. We're going to have a splashing good time; how could one not get involved!

Fort Nelson continues to be home for myself, and Sandy my wife of over 27 years, and a great place to raise our three children, Alisha, Austin and Perry.

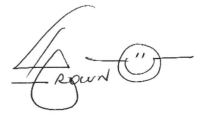

Photo by Anick

# AUTUMN IMAGES – NORTHERN BOOKSHELF

## "THIS WAS NO FRIGGING PICNIC"
(Alaska Highway Construction Tales)
By John T Schmidt
"Without a doubt the best human interest account of the 1942-45 period on the market." Written after 30 years of collecting first hand memories and anecdotes from over 100 different folks involved in all aspects of the Alaska Highway's construction. Varied and colorful characters – a good read.
*(out of print – about 200 copies on hand)*          **$18.95**

## ALCAN TRAILBLAZERS (The Original)
In 1942, U.S. engineers blazed their way through Canadian wilderness, marking a trail to help build the Alaska Highway.  They were the men of 'A' company 648th Engineer topographic battalion. This is their story, as told in their own words, with over 100 photos, maps and drawings. Exploding latrines, lasso'd bears, and more.
*(Out of print – about 150 copies on hand)*          **$14.95**

## THE TRAIL OF '42 – A PICTORIAL HISTORY OF THE ALASKA HIGHWAY.
By Stan Cohen.
*(Over 150,000 copies sold)*
An excellent collection of highway construction images including the arduous battle of mud, muskeg and mosquitoes. Covers some of the early highway proposed routes, the supply routes, bridge projects and communities along the way.          **$14.95**

## THE FORGOTTEN WAR – VOL I

**A pictorial history  -  By Stan Cohen**
The first of four volumes of a comprehensive illustrated history of World War II and its impact on Alaska and Northwest Canada.  This volume  details battles in the Aleutian Islands between  the Americans and the Japanese.                                     **$29.95**

## THE FORGOTTEN WAR - VOL II

**A pictorial history  -  By Stan Cohen**
The second of four volumes of a comprehensive illustrated history of World War II and its impact on Alaska and Northwest Canada.  This volume  details the construction of the Canol Highway & Pipeline from Norman Wells NWT to Whitehorse.      **$29.95**

## ALCAN & CANOL – A Pictorial History of
**Two Great World War II Construction Projects.**
**By Stan Cohen**
Anyone who travels the Alaska Highway today for the first time would be hard put to imagine the hardships associated with the building of the road. In the early 1940's this was mostly wilderness, traveled by a small band of hunters, trappers and prospectors and several Indian tribes.  This anniversary edition is the definitive photo history of the Alaska Highway (Alcan) and CANOL projects.                                     **$34.95**

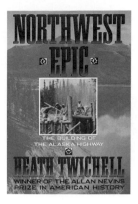

## NORTHWEST EPIC – The Building of the Alaska Highway
### By Heath Twichell
*(Hard cover - autographed copies!)*
A superb sweeping and richly textured history, that tells the dramatic story of courageous U.S. Army Engineers and civilian contractors who toiled to build a 1500 mile emergency supply line through rugged Canadian wilderness to isolated military bases in Alaska. Original photos, maps and illustrations- over 40 pages of notes, bibliography and index.*(An excellent book)* *(Out of print - only 20 copies available)*            **$90.00**

## THE WORLD WAR II BLACK REGIMENT THAT HELPED BUILD THE ALASKA HIGHWAY:
### A Photographic History.
### ©2002: By William E Griggs, edited by Philip J Merrill
A rich treasure of previously unpublished black and white photos by the official regimental photographer for the 97th Engineers Battalion to document their work in Alaska. *(Hardcover)*            **$42.95**

## WINGS OVER THE ALASKA HIGHWAY –
### A photographic History of Aviation on the Alaska Highway.
### ©2001: By Bruce McAllister
"...have captured the real essence of what aviation is all about. These heart stopping adventures in the Far North are made all the more real, thanks to the extraordinary photography that accompanies the text." *(Softcover)*            **$44.95**

## THE MILEPOST – Trip planner for Alaska, Yukon and Northwest Territories, British Columbia and Alberta.

Since 1949, the "bible of North country travel." Nearly 800 pages Updated annually by a team of seasoned editors covering mile-by-mile logs of 30 major routes and 60 side trips. Includes pull-out MILEPOST Plan-a-trip map, mileage charts, ferry schedules, and more than 500 color photos. "The quintessential reference"- Associated Press. "I love the Milepost! No one should consider an Alaska trip without a current issue." – Mark Victor Hansen

$34.95

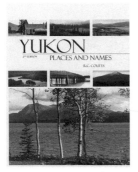

## YUKON PLACES AND NAMES
### By R. C. Coutts

Revised, expanded and reprinted 2003, Yukon Places and Names is an excellent source of information on well over a thousand places and presents fascinating accounts of their history and biography. It is a reference book, a travel guide and a joy for the armchair explorer.

$24.95

## Tales of a Catskinner - A personal Account of Building the Alaska Highway, The Winter Trail, and Canol Pipeline Road in 1942-43
### By Chester L Russell

Chester Russell tells the amazing story of how he and 14000 other soldiers just like him ended up working under god-awful conditions in the wilds of western Canada and Alaska to build the Alaska Highway and the CANOL Project during the early years of WW II. If you like your history up close and personal, this is the book for you.

$19.95

## ALASKA HIGHWAY 1942-1992   VHS

Pushed though in eight months of 1942 as
a wilderness trail, and completed in just two
years, the Alcan travels within some of the
most beautiful, yet forbidding in North America.
This excellent video includes archival and
contemporary footage to show the significance of
construction achievement.
*(Running time 58 minutes)*                    **$39.95**

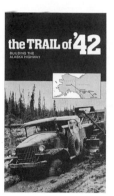

## THE TRAIL OF '42   VHS

Travel on a trip along the famous Alaska Highway,
stretching from Dawson Creek, BC to Delta Junction,
Alaska and continuing to Fairbanks, Alaska, a distance
over 1500 miles.  This tape traces the history using
contemporary footage, interviews and still photos.
*(Running time 60 minutes)*                    **$34.95**

## SO...YOU WANT TO KNOW MORE ABOUT FORT NELSON...EH?   VHS

Visit Fort Nelson, BC Canada located at mile 300
on the Alaska Highway for an all season look at the
community and area at work and at play, viewed
through the camera lens of a resident photographer
Earl L. Brown.
*(Running time 25 minutes)*                    **$22.95**

# AUTUMN IMAGES – NORTHERN BOOKSHELF

# TO ORDER

**MAIL IT!**                     Box 904-T
                                 Fort Nelson, BC
                                 Canada  V0C 1R0

**FAX IT!**                      250-774-6767

**PHONE IT!**                    250-774-3488
*(Have your Visa or Mastercard ready)*

**TOLL FREE!**                   1-877-645-3767

**CHECK OUT OUR WEBSITE**        www.autumnimages.com
(Watch for website specials)

## IMPORTANT ORDERING INFORMATION
## (All prices in Canadian Funds)

SHIPPING AND HANDLING CHARGES

| FOR ORDERS | (SURFACE RATE)<br>TO CANADA | TO USA |
|---|---|---|
| $ 25.00 or less | $ 5.00 | $ 7.00 |
| 25.01 – 50.00 | 7.00 | 9.00 |
| 50.01 – 75.00 | 8.00 | 10.00 |
| 75.01 – 100.00 | 9.00 | 12.00 |
| 100.01 – 150.00 | 10.00 | 13.50 |
| 150.01 – 200.00 | 12.00 | 16.00 |
| 200.01 – 300.00 | 15.00 | 19.00 |
| 300.00 or more | FREE | 10.00 |

**RUSH ORDERS BY PHONE ONLY –
WE'LL BE GLAD TO HELP YOU!**

**CALL FOR DETAILS AND COSTS.**

# ORDER FORM - PLEASE PRINT

Name: _____

Address: _____

City: _____     Province/State: _____

Country: _____     Postal/Zip Code: _____

Telephone: _____     E-mail: _____

| Title | # Copies | Each | Total |
|-------|----------|------|-------|
| Alcan Trail Blazers - A.H. Forgotten Heros | | $  19.95 | $ |
| This Was No Friggin' Picnic | | 18.95 | |
| Alcan Trailblazers - (The Original) | | 14.95 | |
| The Trail of '42 | | 14.95 | |
| The Forgotten War - Vol I | | 29.95 | |
| The Forgotten War - Vol II | | 29.95 | |
| Alcan and Canol | | 34.95 | |
| Northwest Epic (Autographed) | | 90.00 | |
| World War II - Black Regiment- Alaska Hwy. | | 42.95 | |
| Wings Over The Alaska Highway | | 44.95 | |
| The Milepost | | 34.95 | |
| Yukon Places and Names | | 24.95 | |
| Tales of a Catskinner | | 19.95 | |
| Alaska Highway 1942-1992  VHS | | 39.95 | |
| Trail of '42  VHS | | 34.95 | |
| So... want to know about Fort Nelson? VHS | | 22.95 | |

|  | |
|--|--|
| **Subtotal** | |
| SAVE MONEY $$$  3 or more titles - Less 20% | |
| **Subtotal** | |
| Canada only -  7% G.S.T. | |
| Shipping & Handling | |
| **Total** | $ |

*All prices are in Canadian dollars*

Payment:      Visa        Mastercard

Card Number: _____

Expiry Date: _____

Signature: _____

Make cheque or money order payable to:
**AUTUMN IMAGES INC.**
**P.O. Box 904-T**
**Fort Nelson, BC  V0C 1R0**

Telephone: 250-774-3488          Fax: 250-774-6767
E-mail: autumn@pris.ca          www.autumnimages.com

# See Over for
# Northern Bookshelf
# Order Form